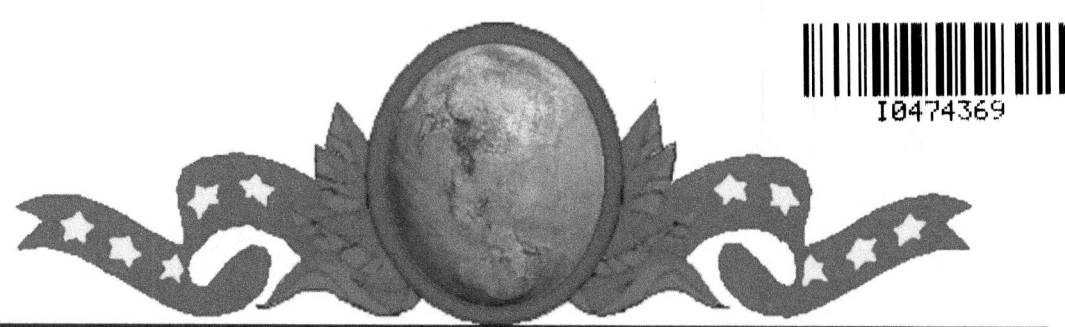

Real World
Colouring Book
For Advanced Users & Adults

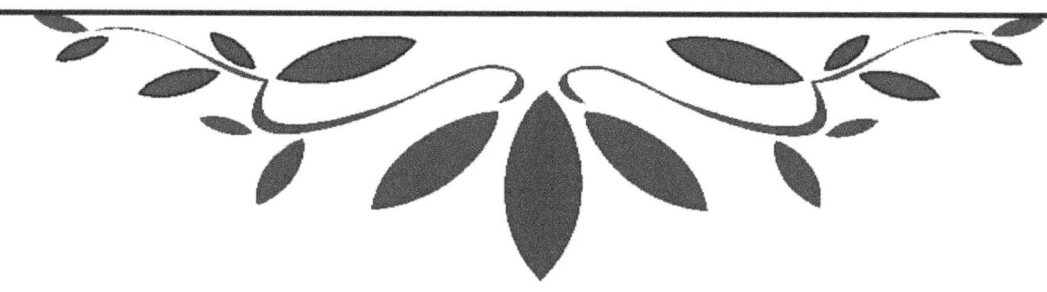

50 Images

Created From Real Life Photos
For You To Colour As You Please.

ISBN 978-0-359-78829-3

Beach Sheds

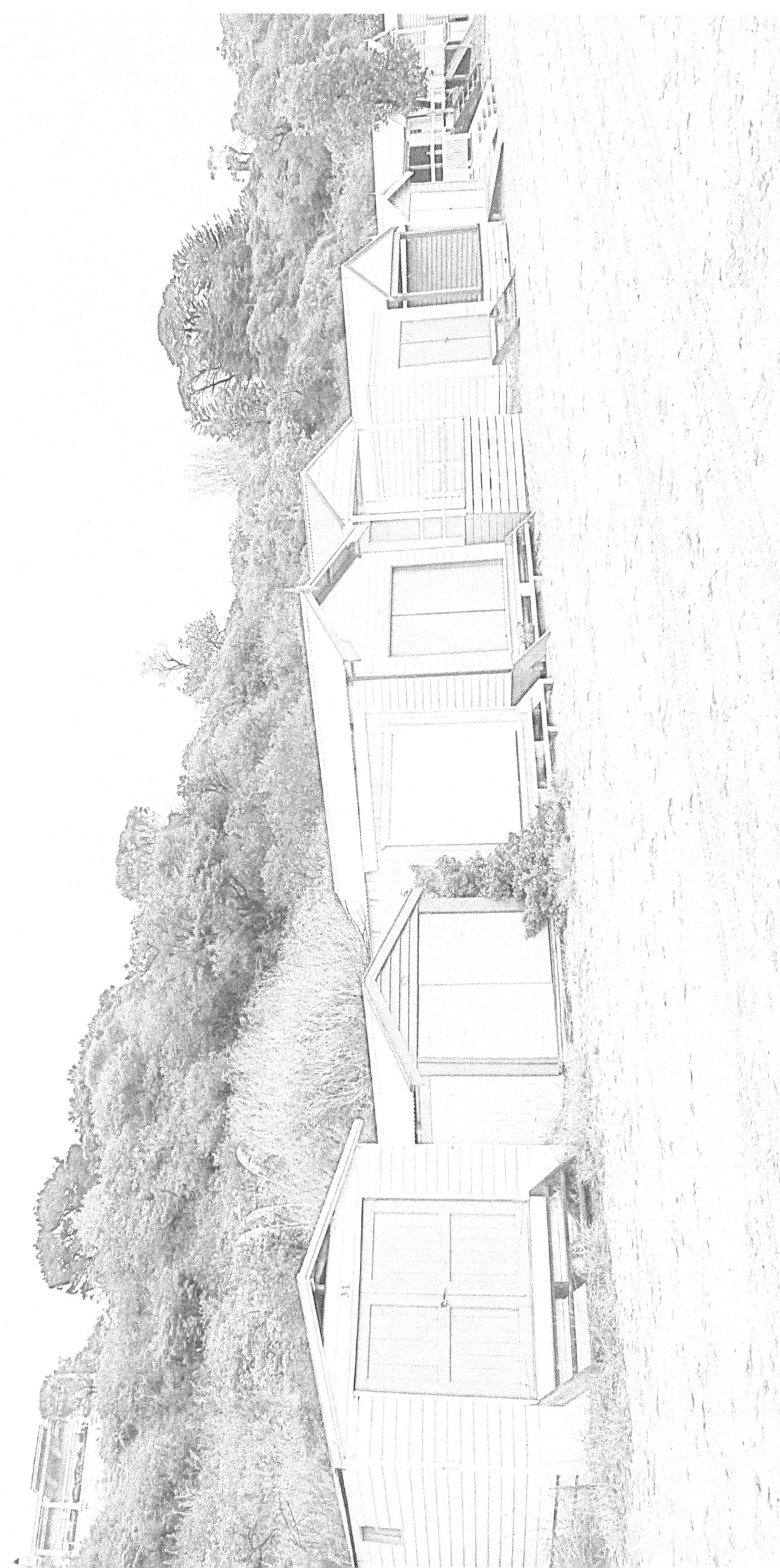

Bear

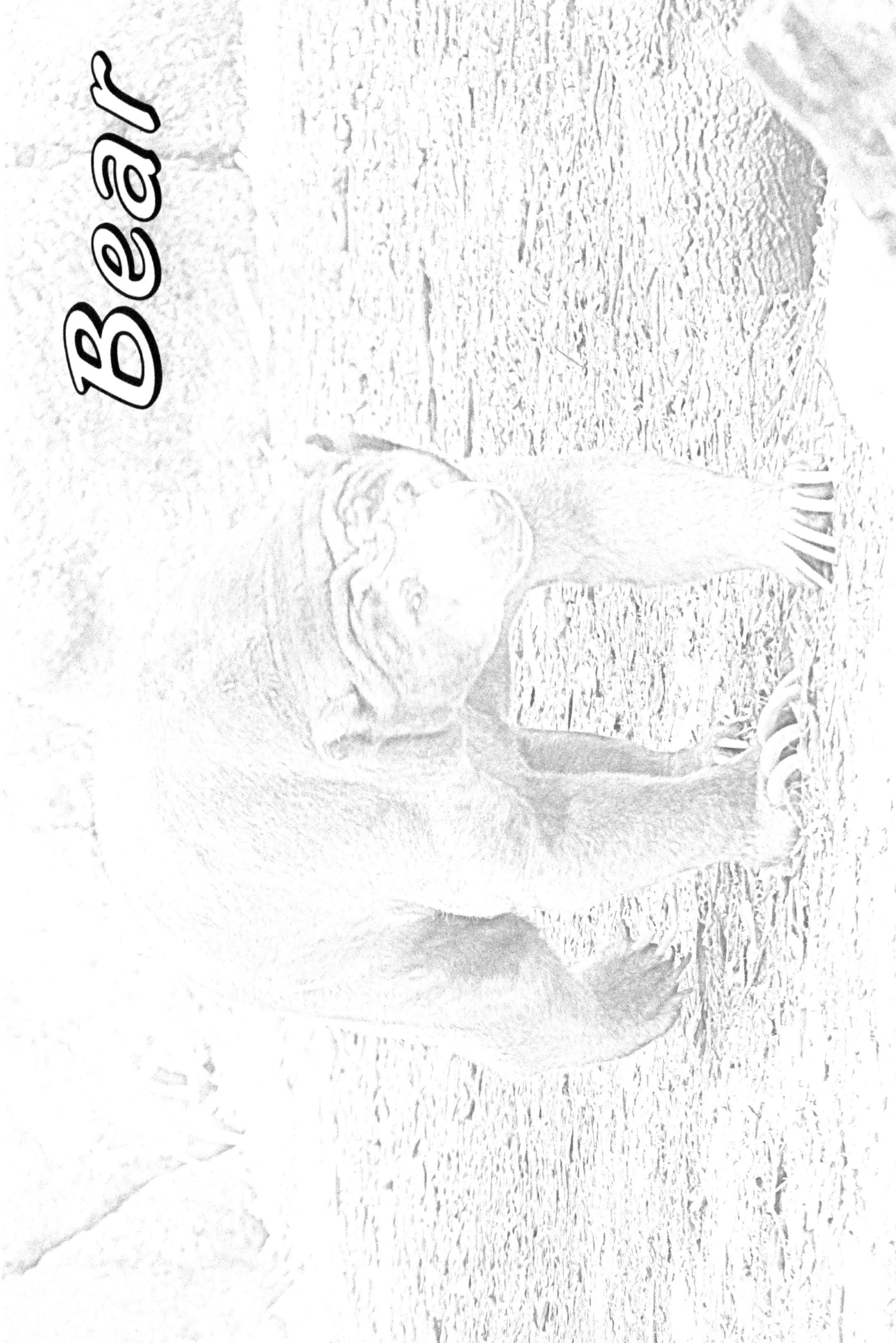

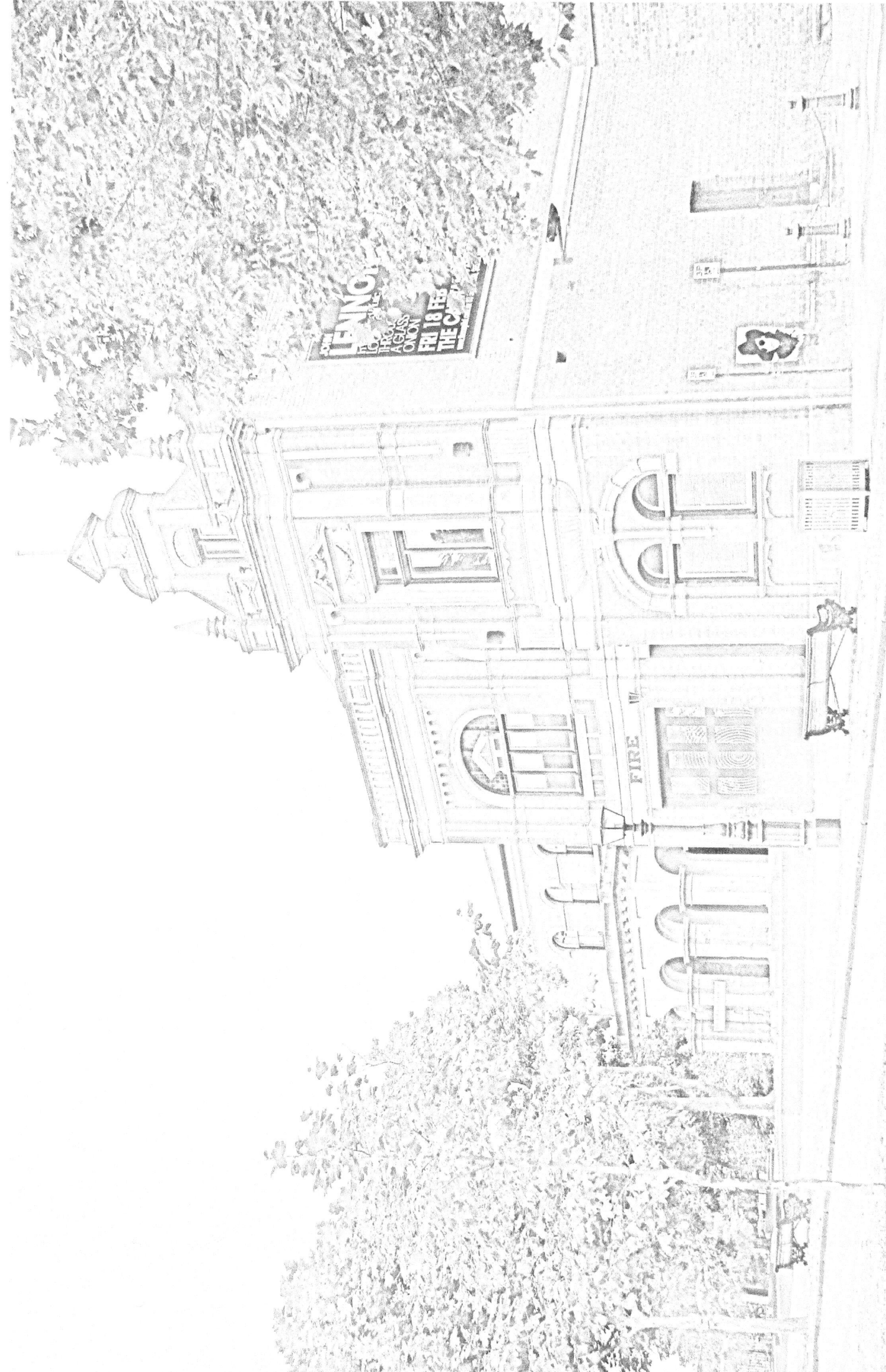

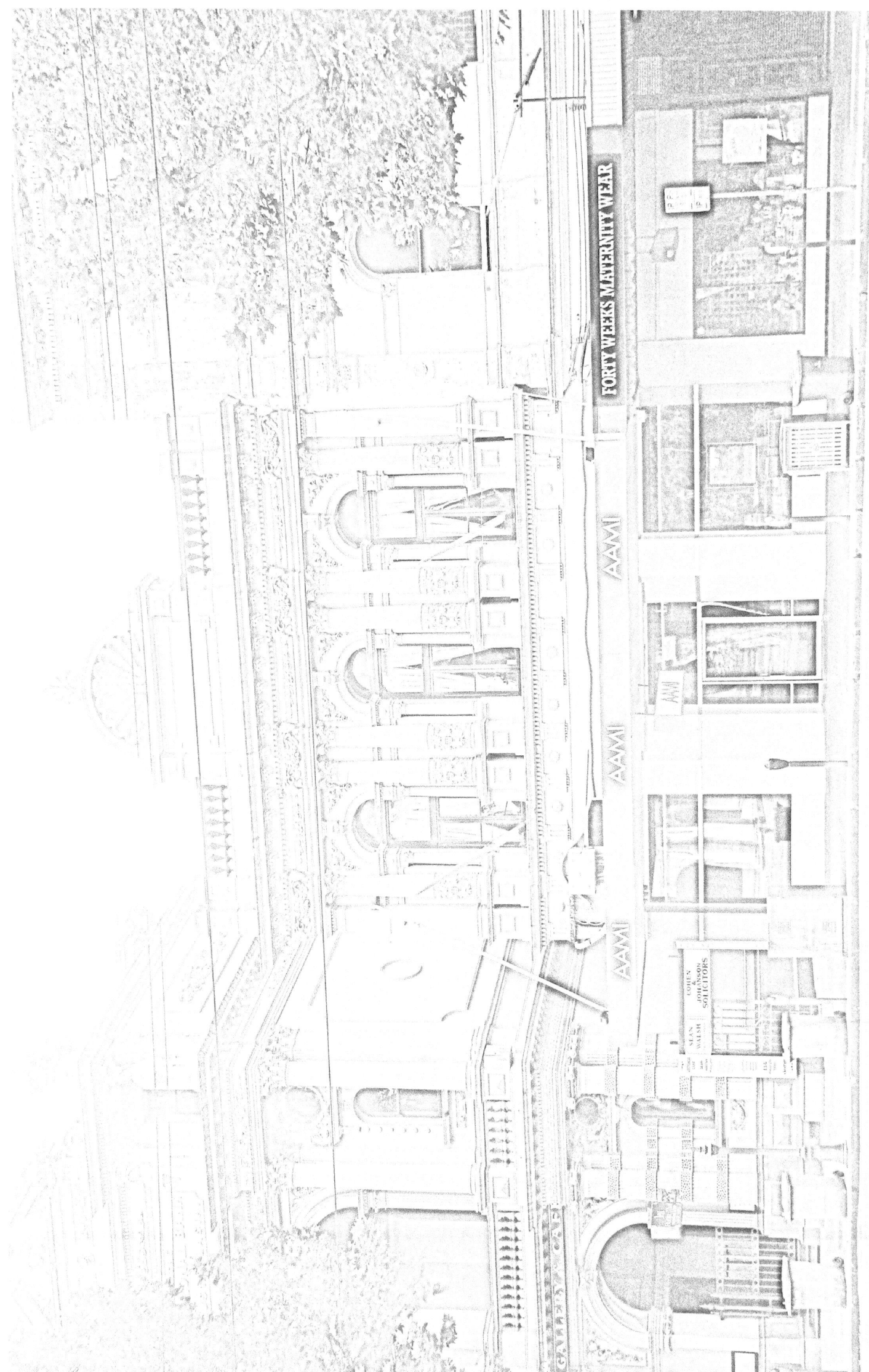

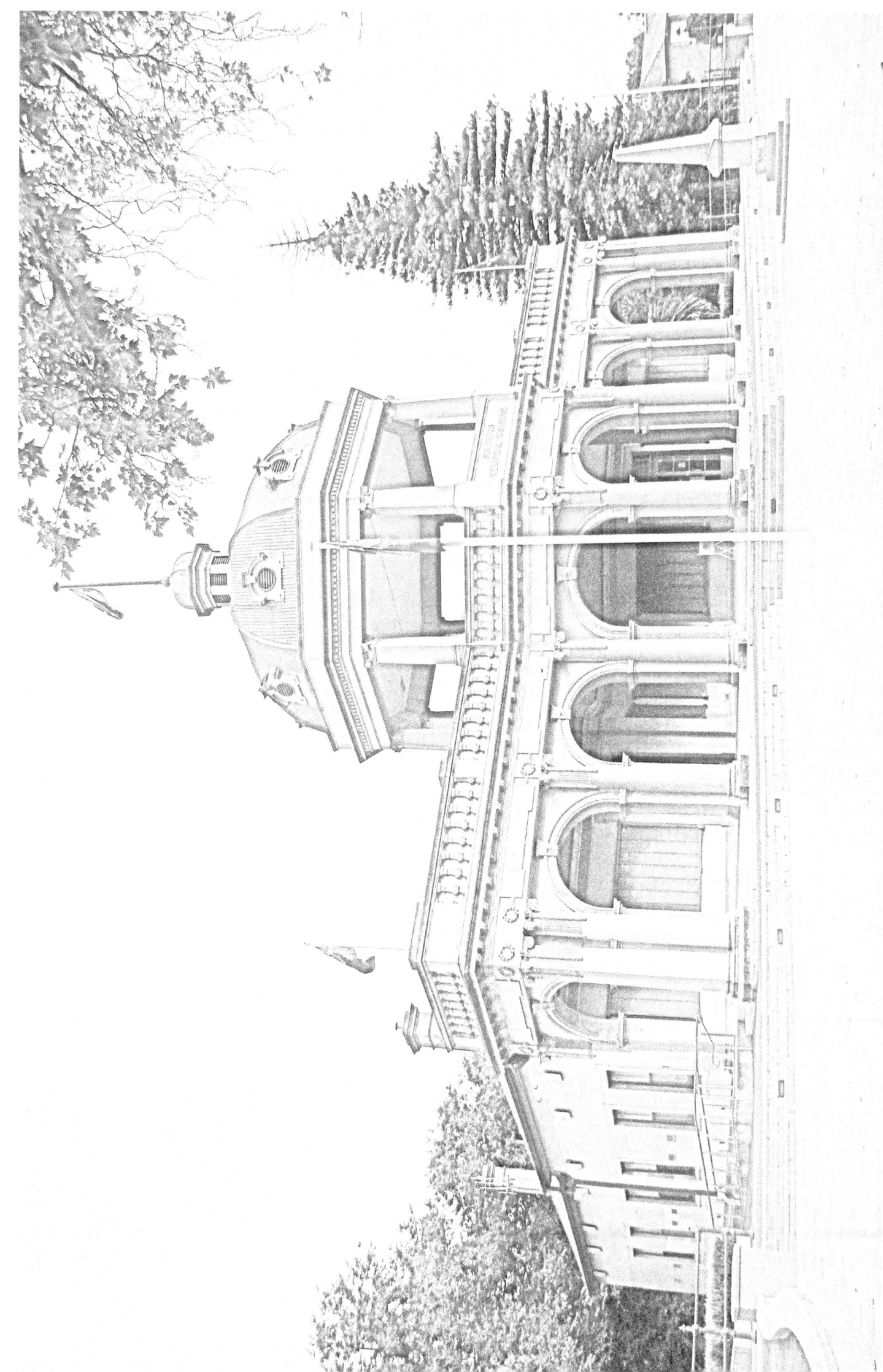

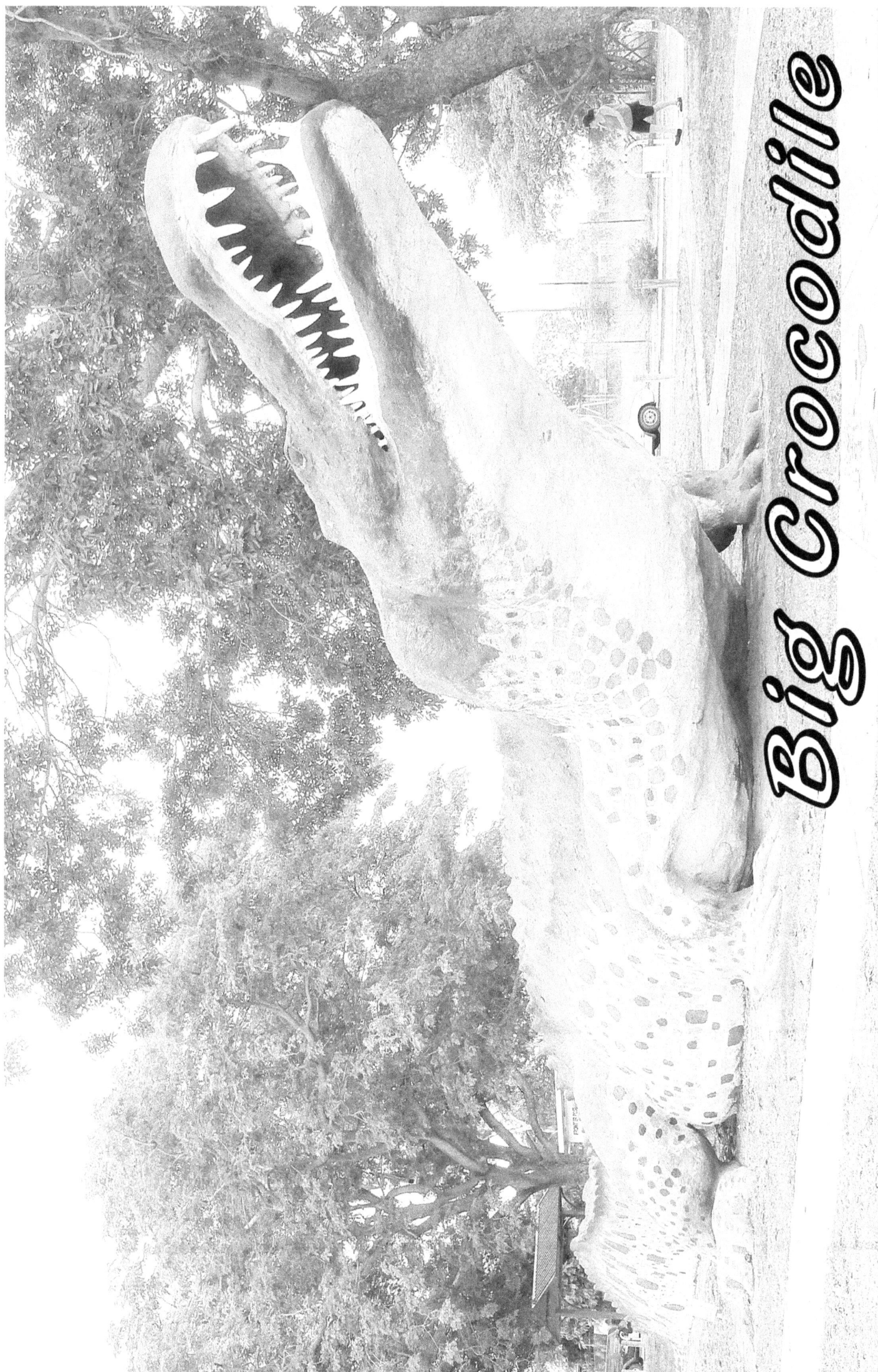

Big Crocodile

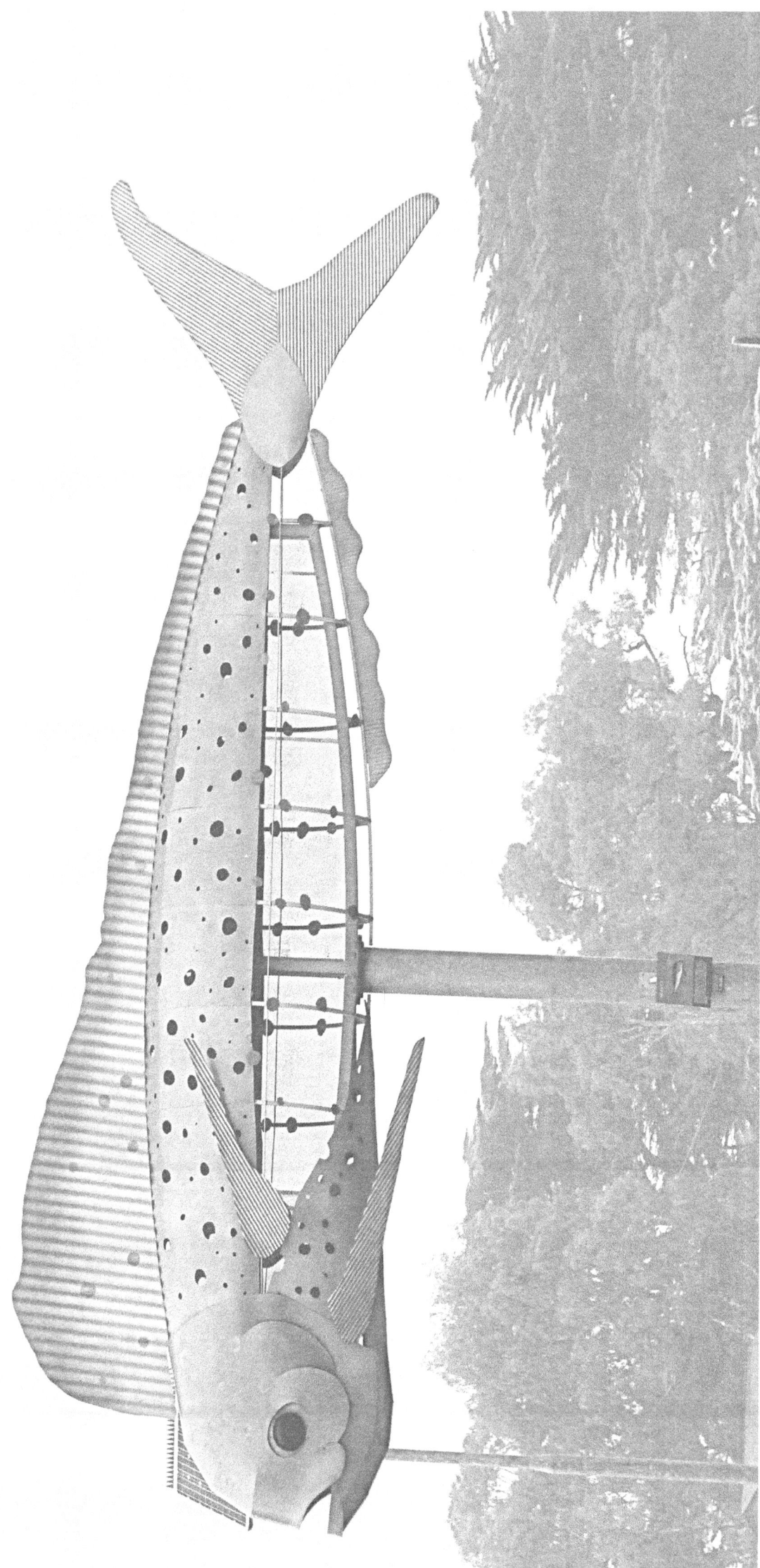

Big Fish

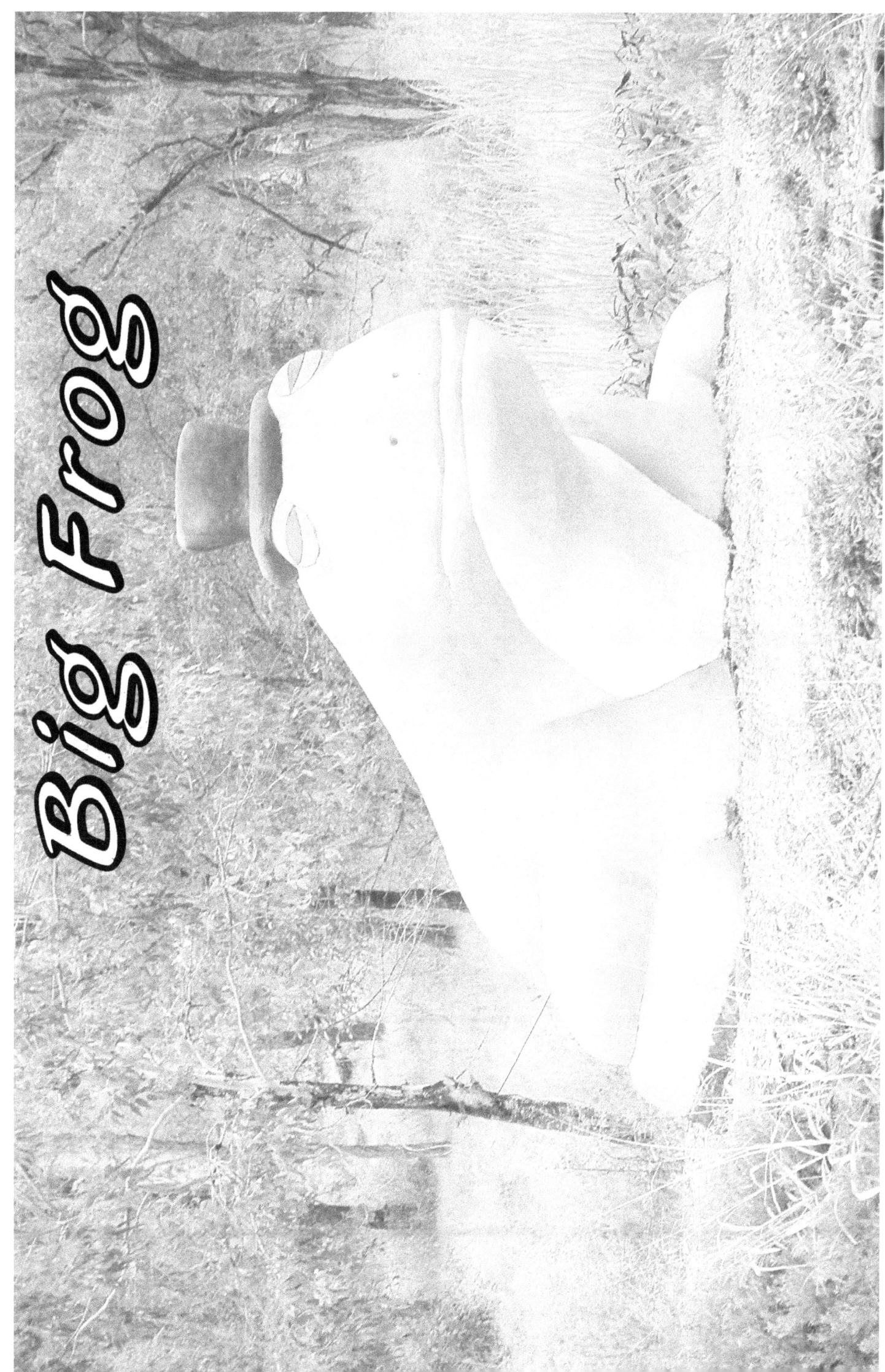

Big Frog

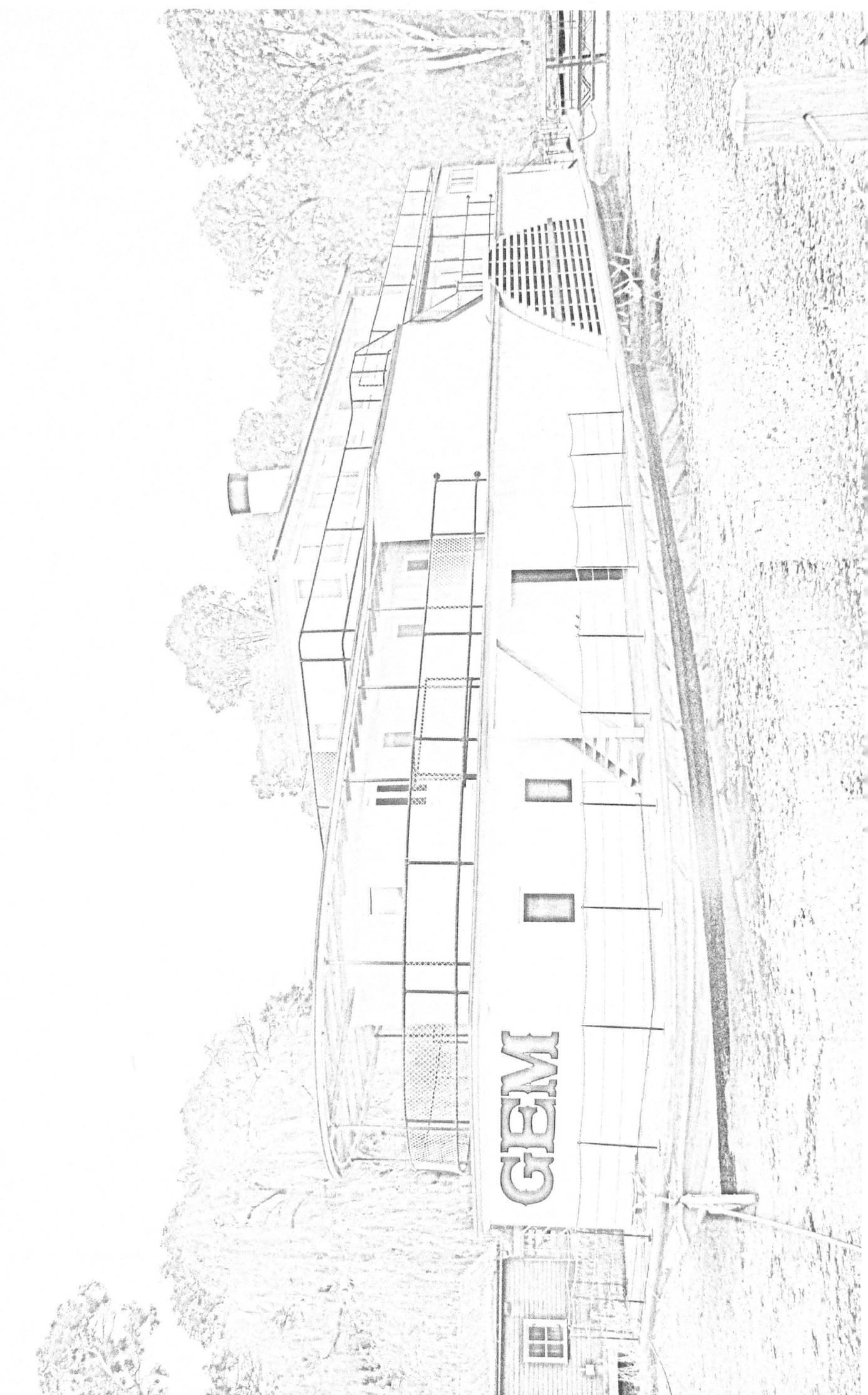

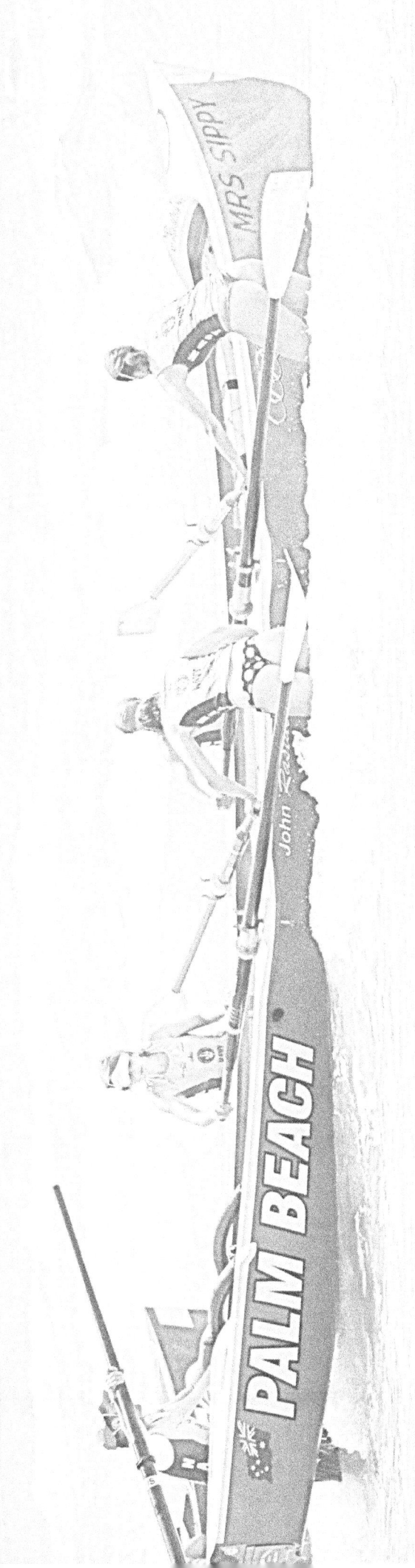

Brush Turkey

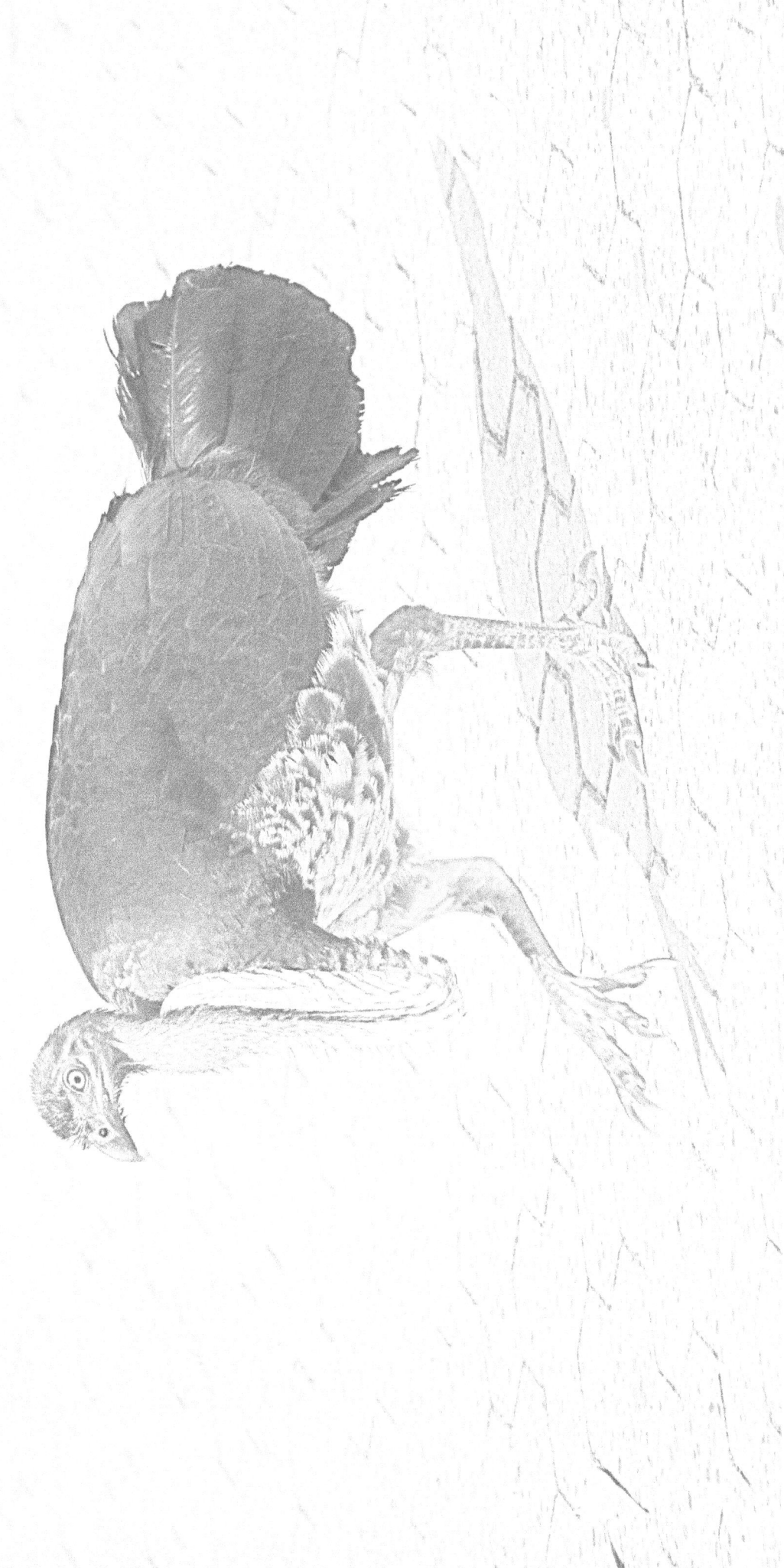

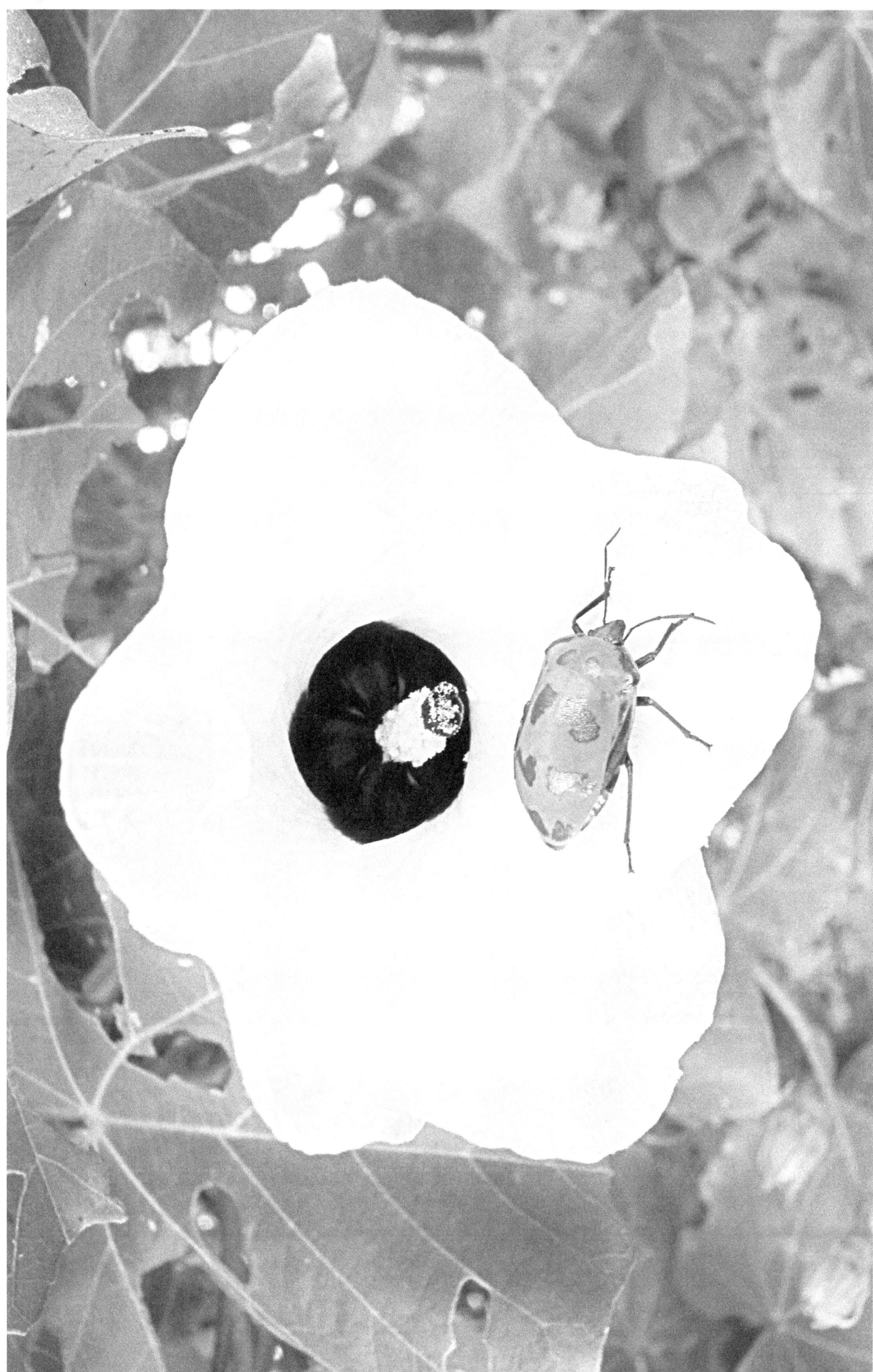

Butterfly

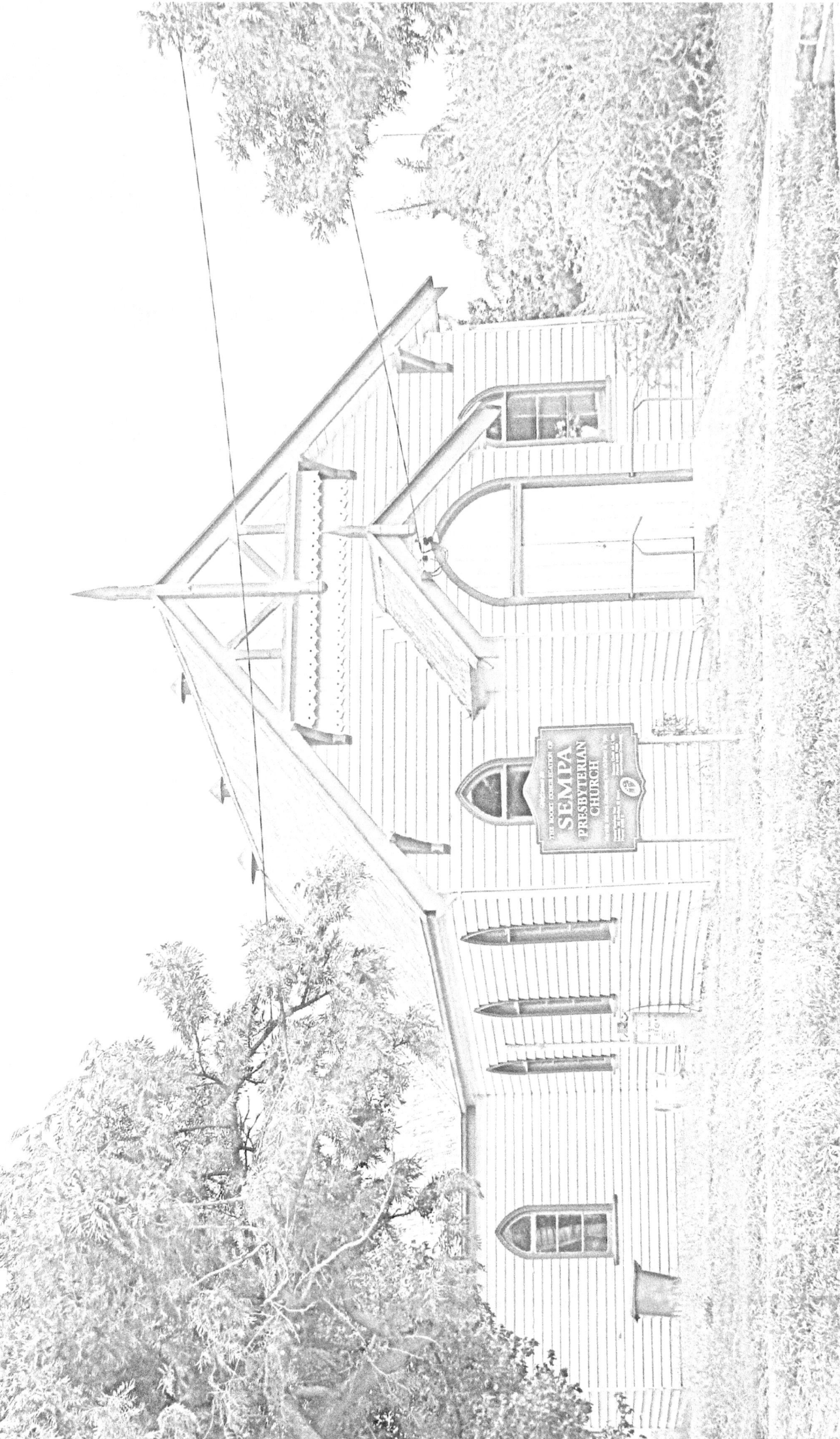

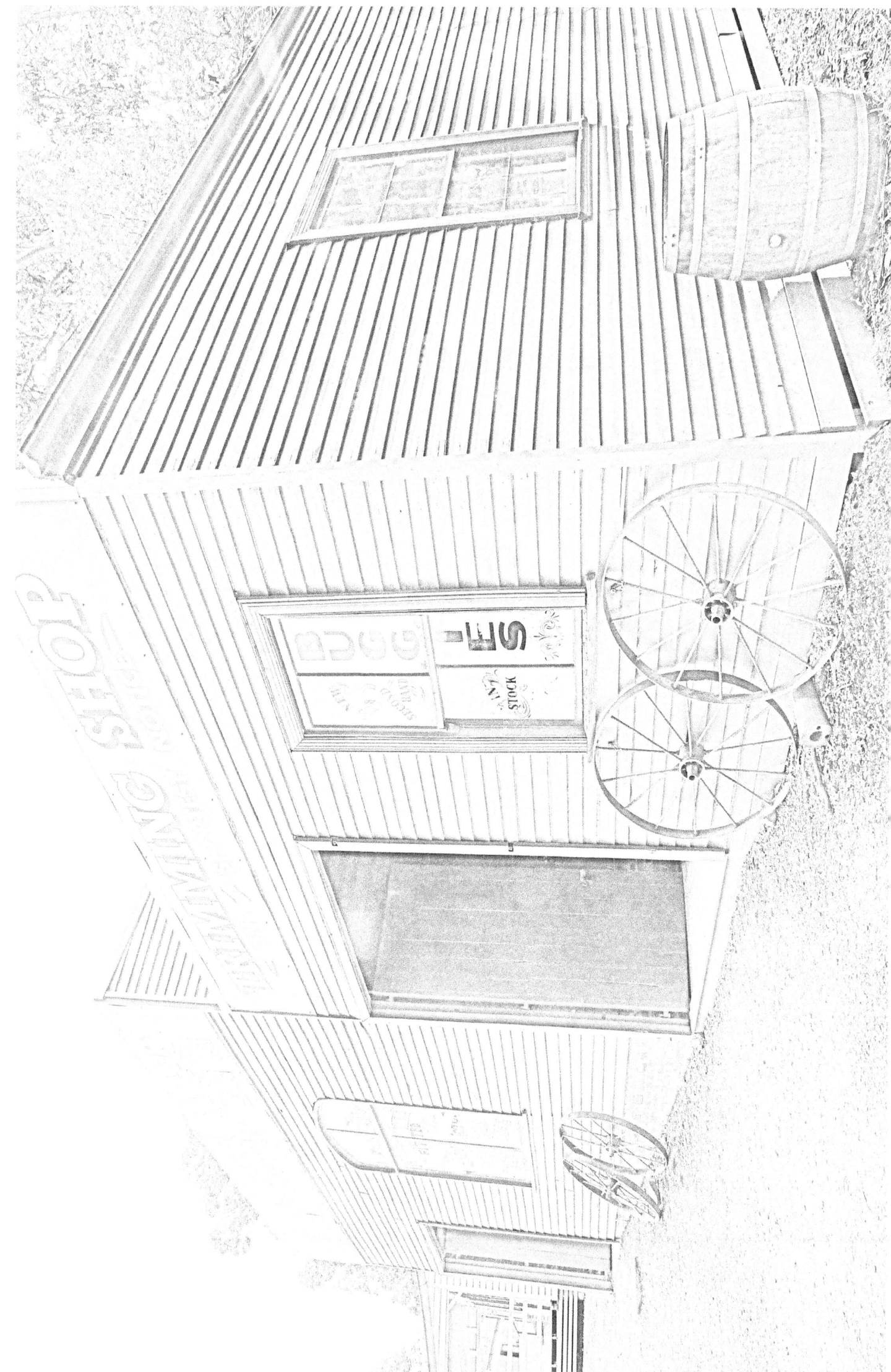

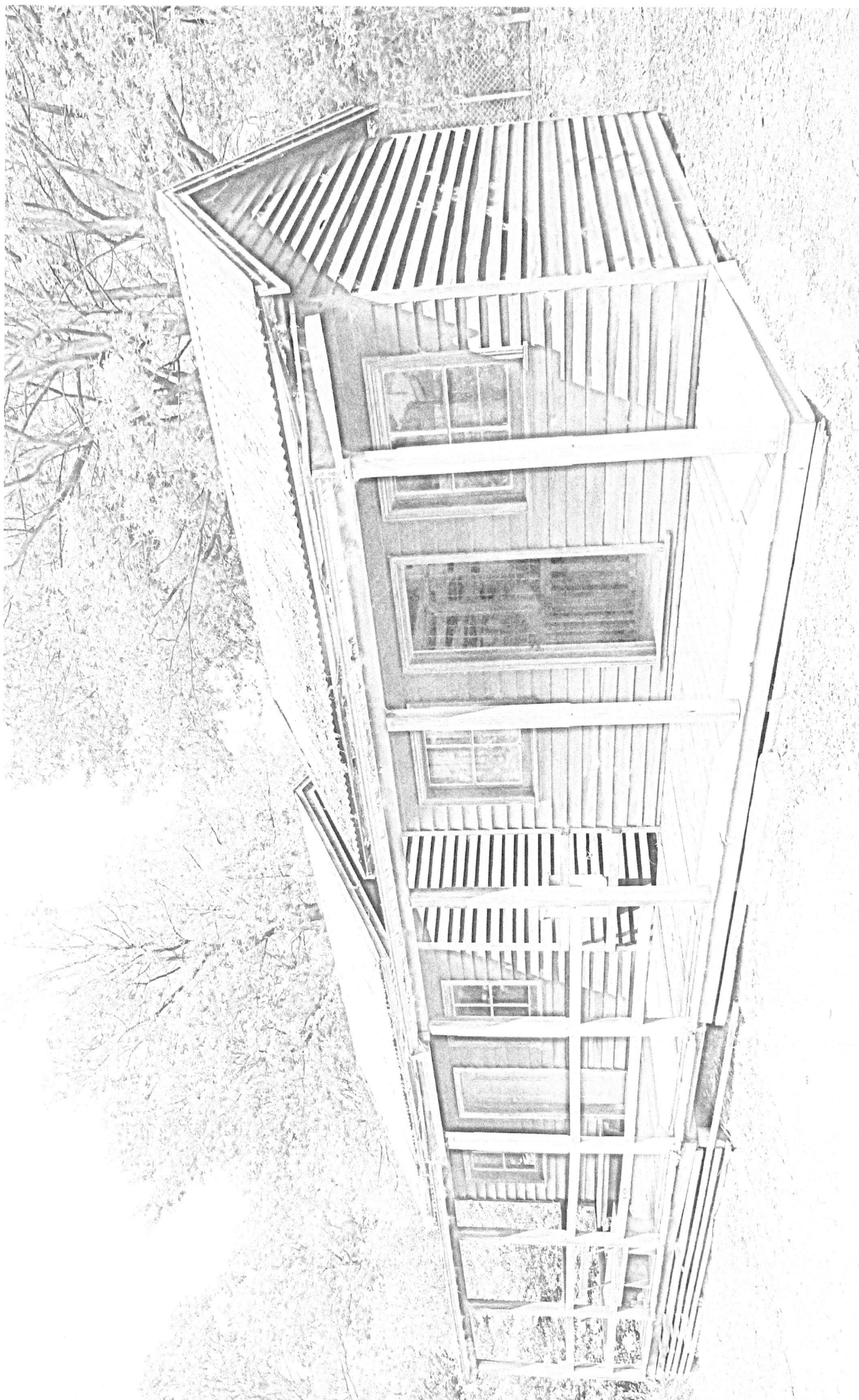

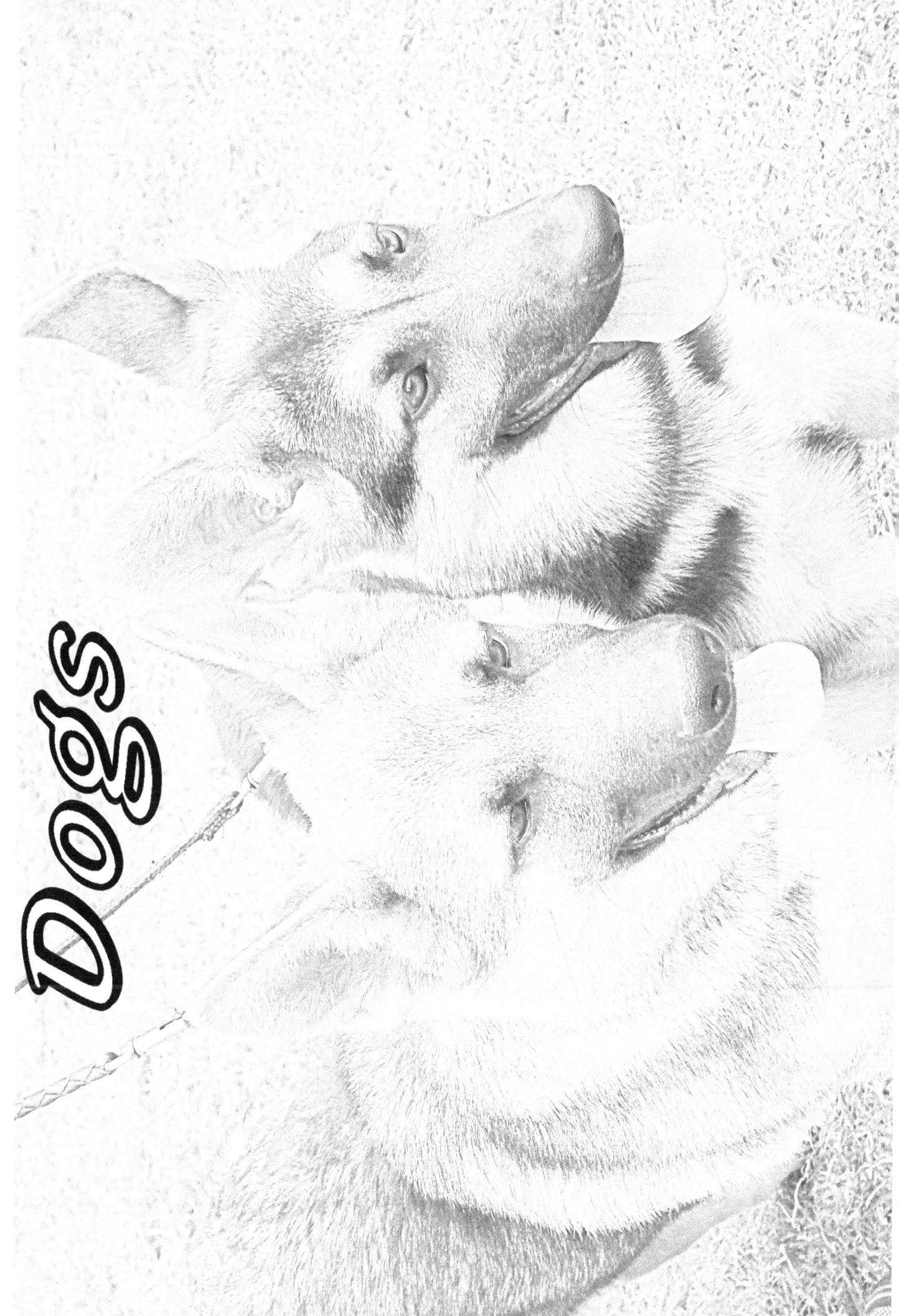

Dogs

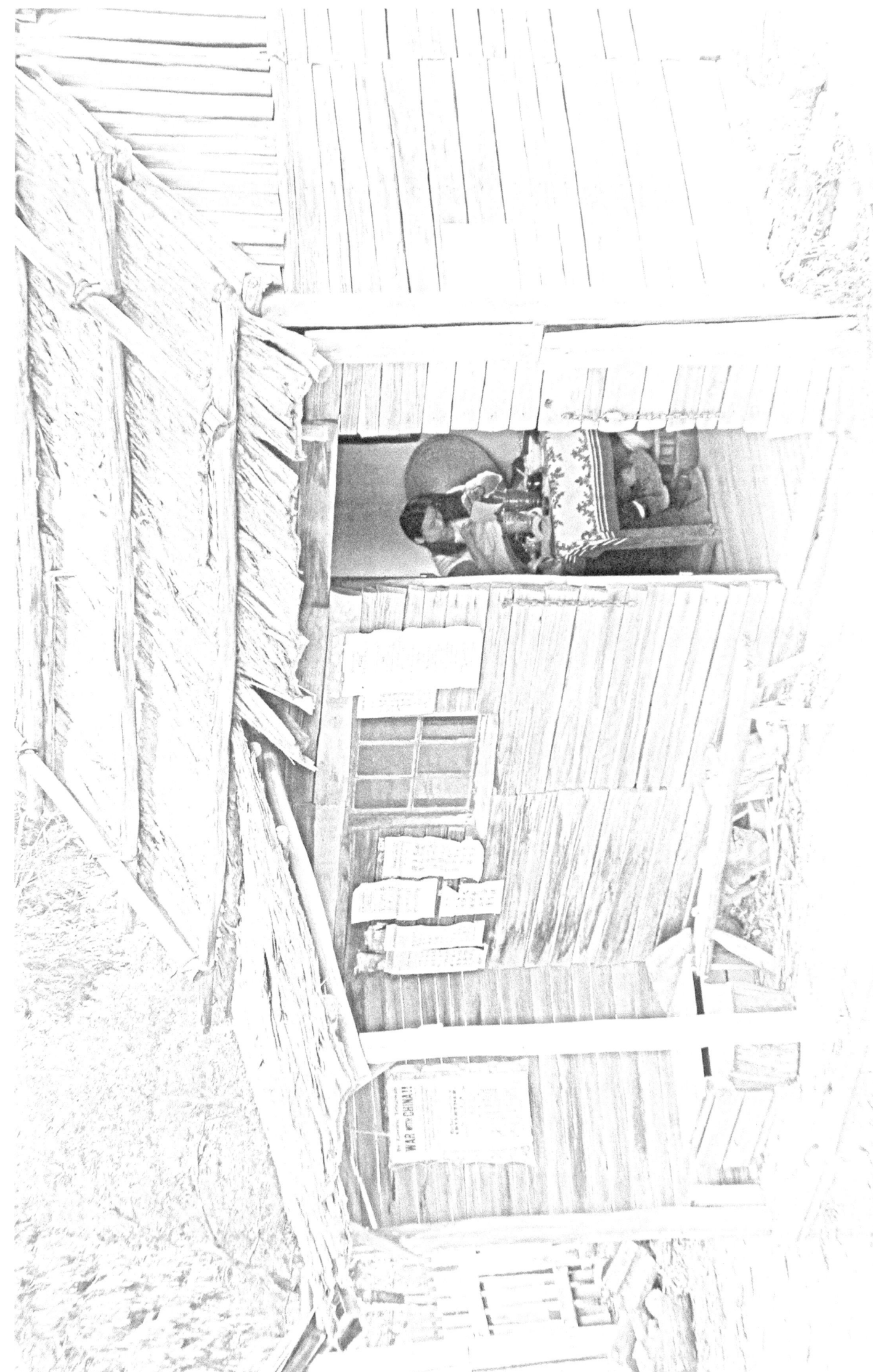

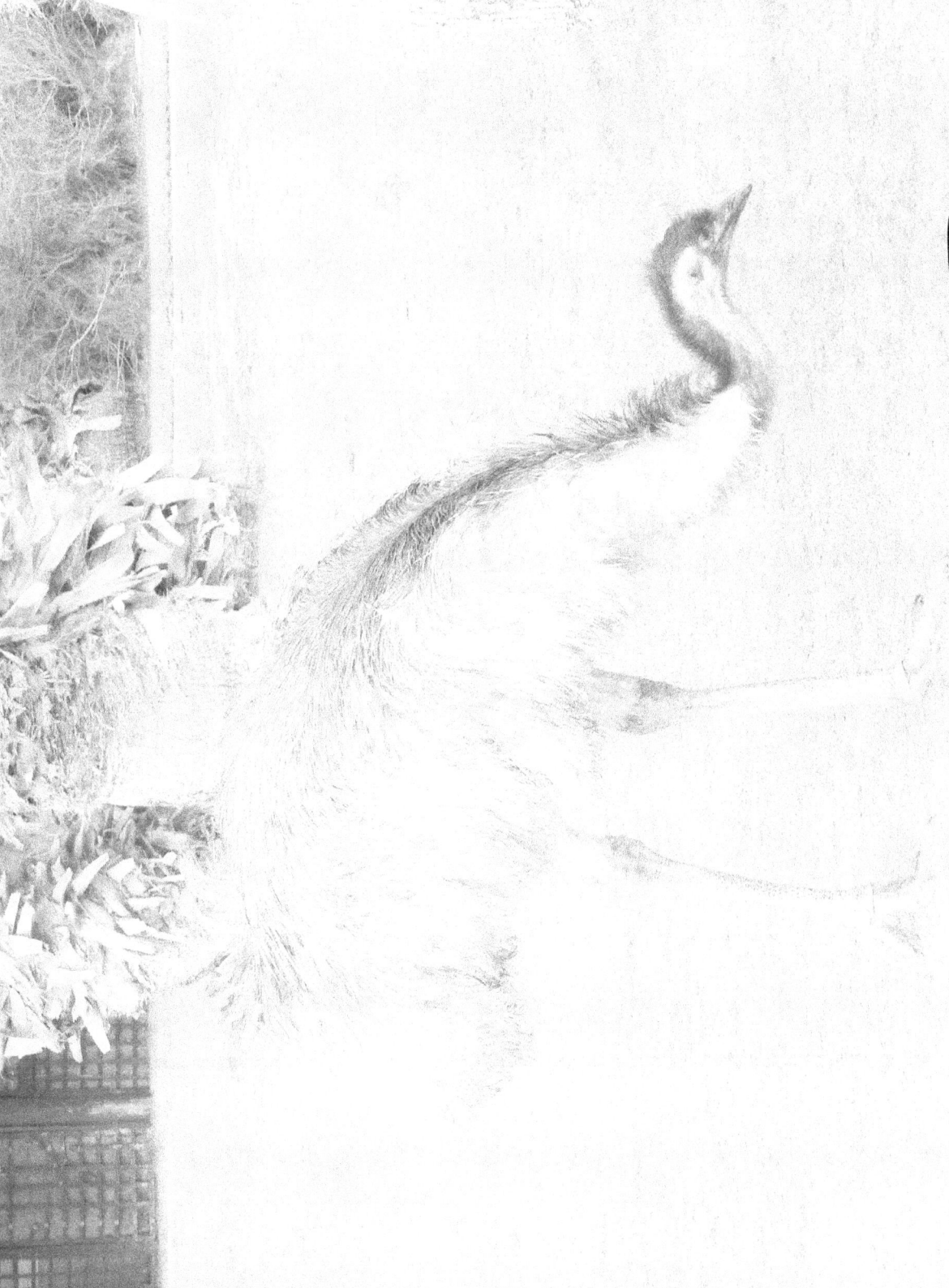

Emu

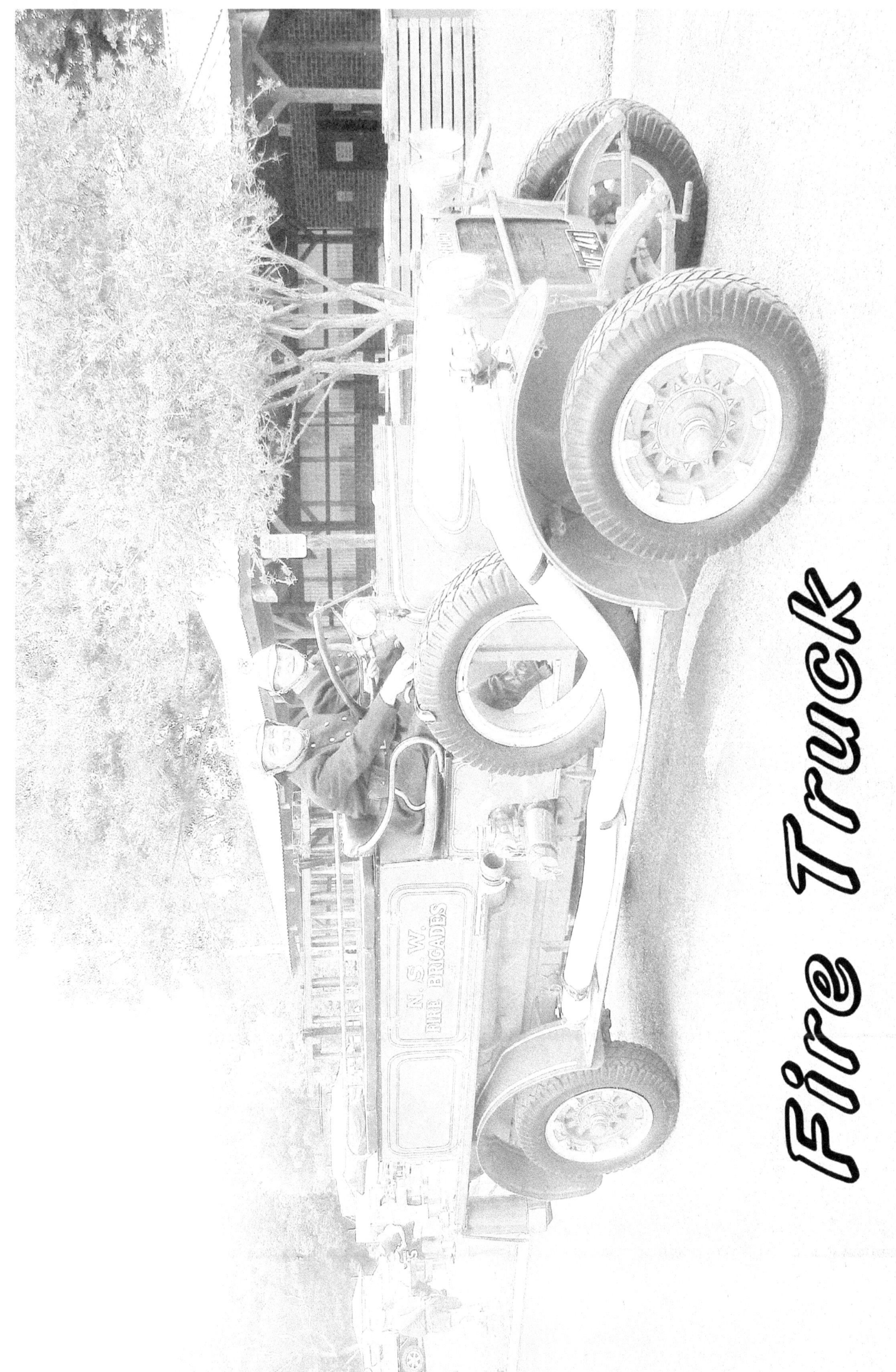

Fire Truck

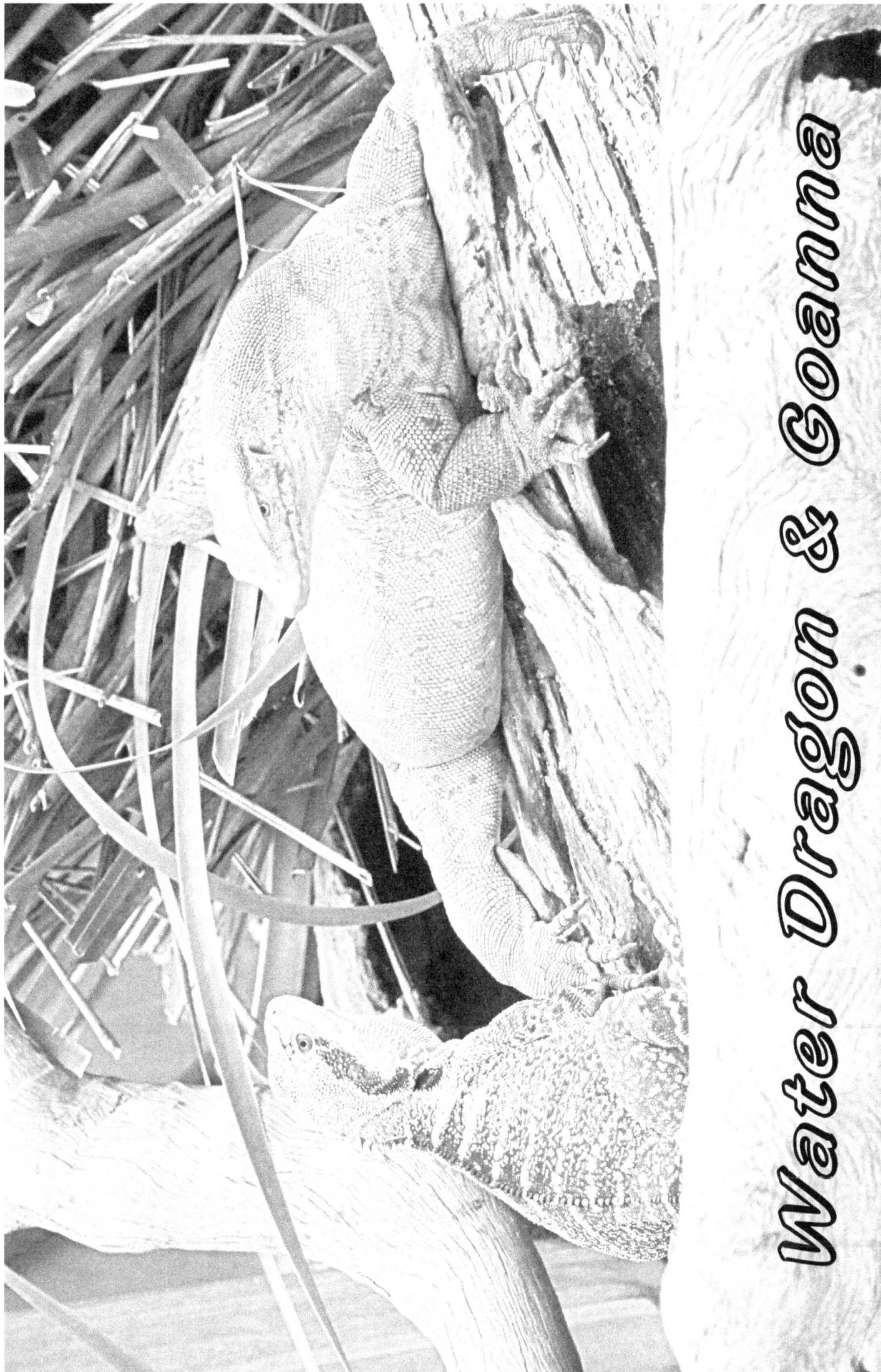

Water Dragon & Goanna

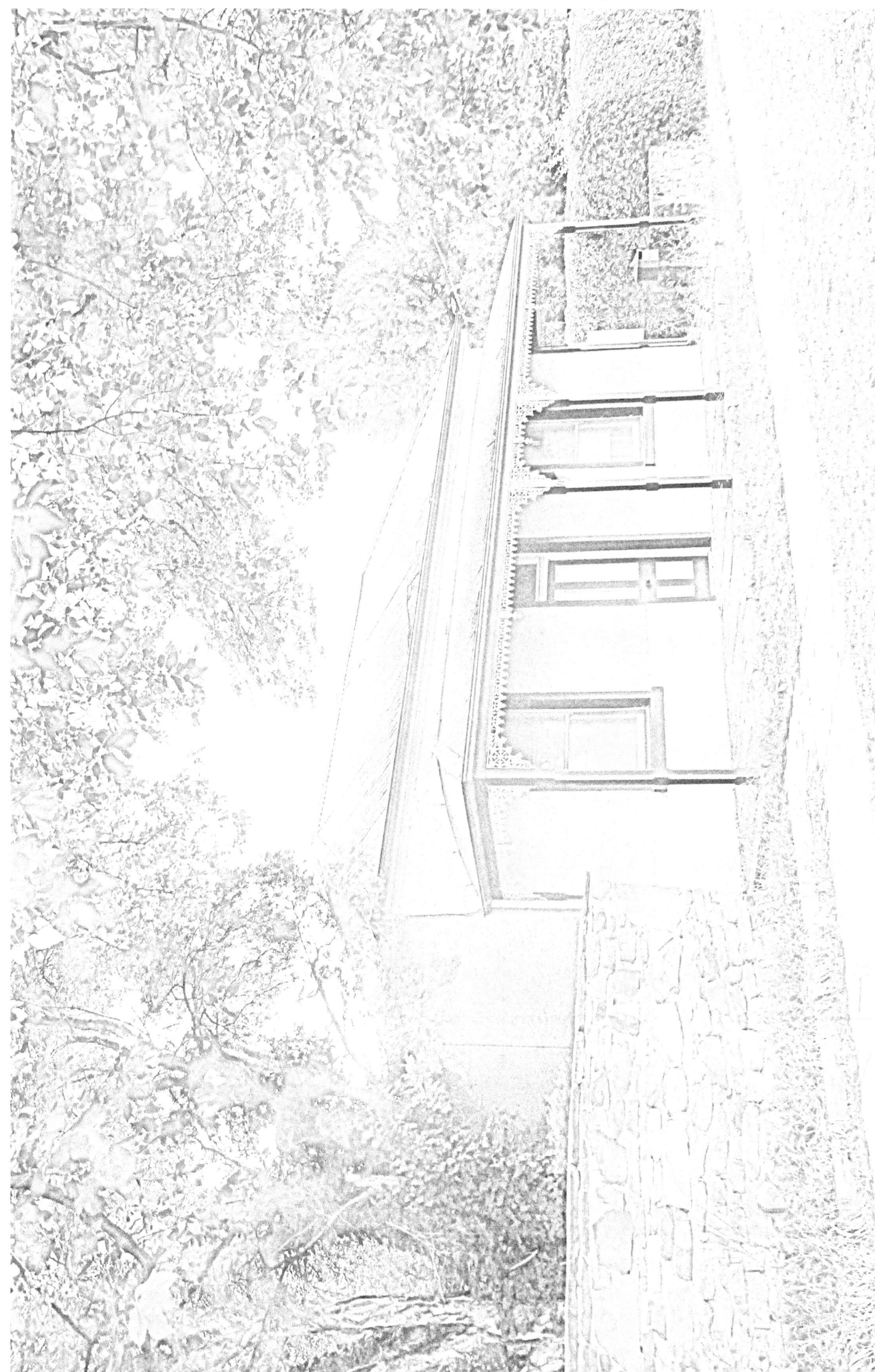

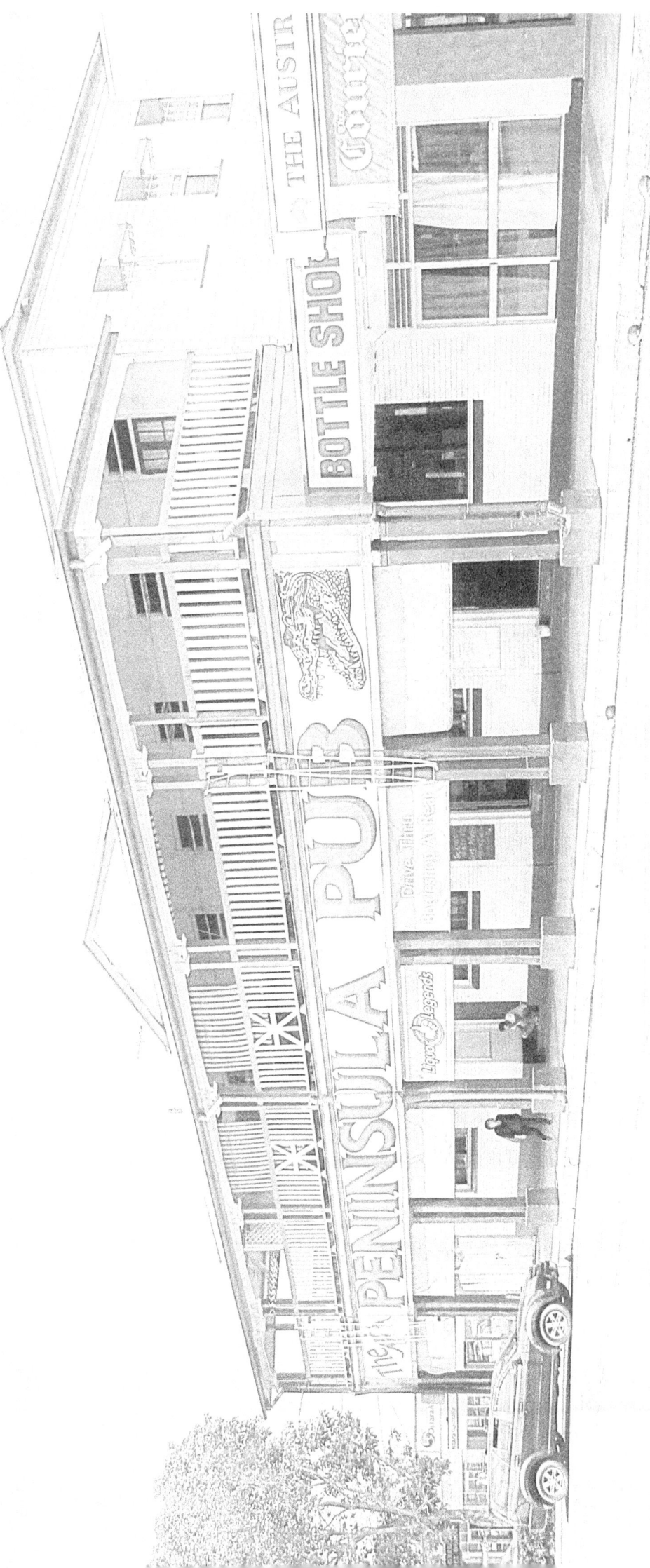

Hotel

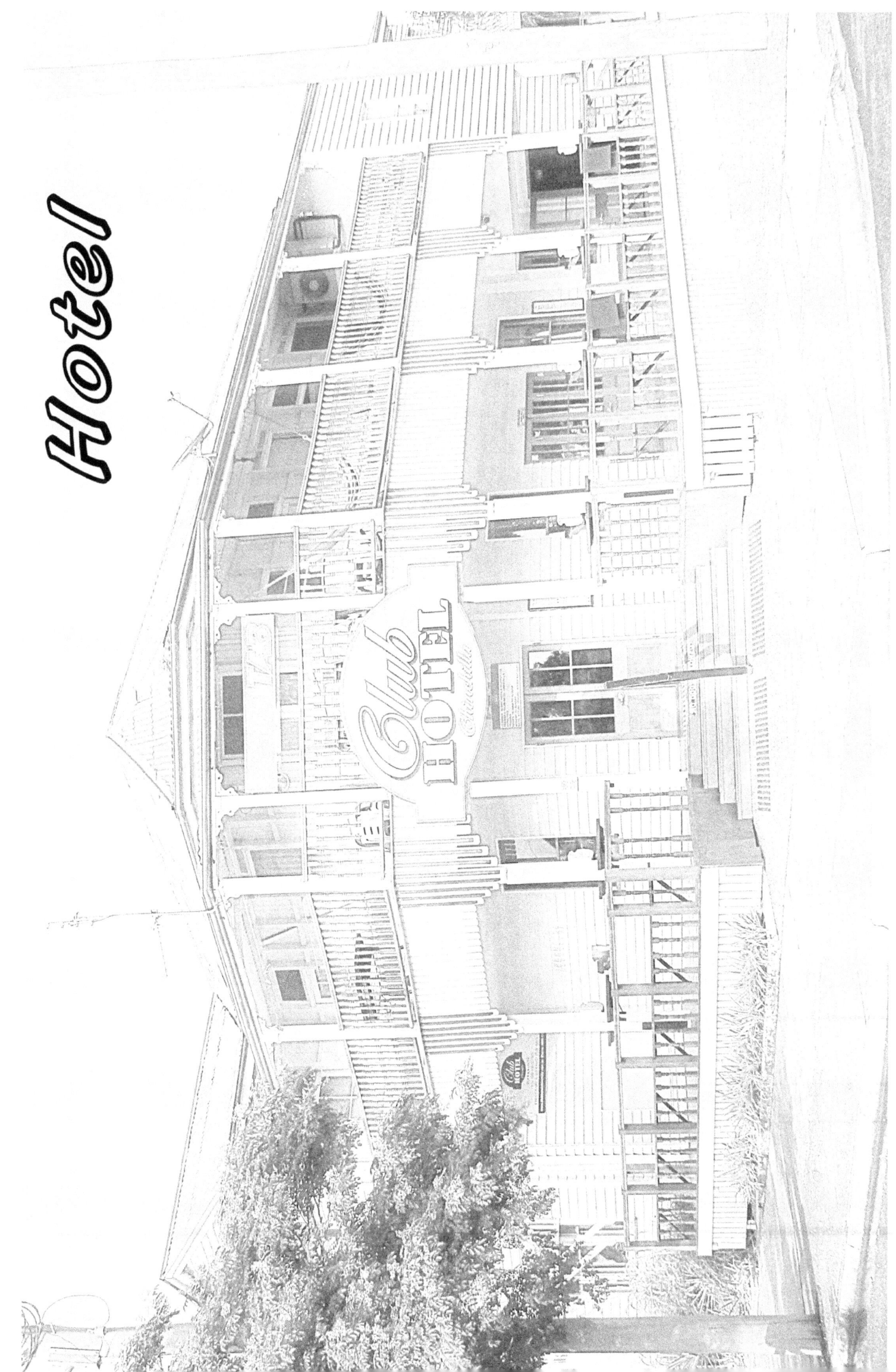

Hotel

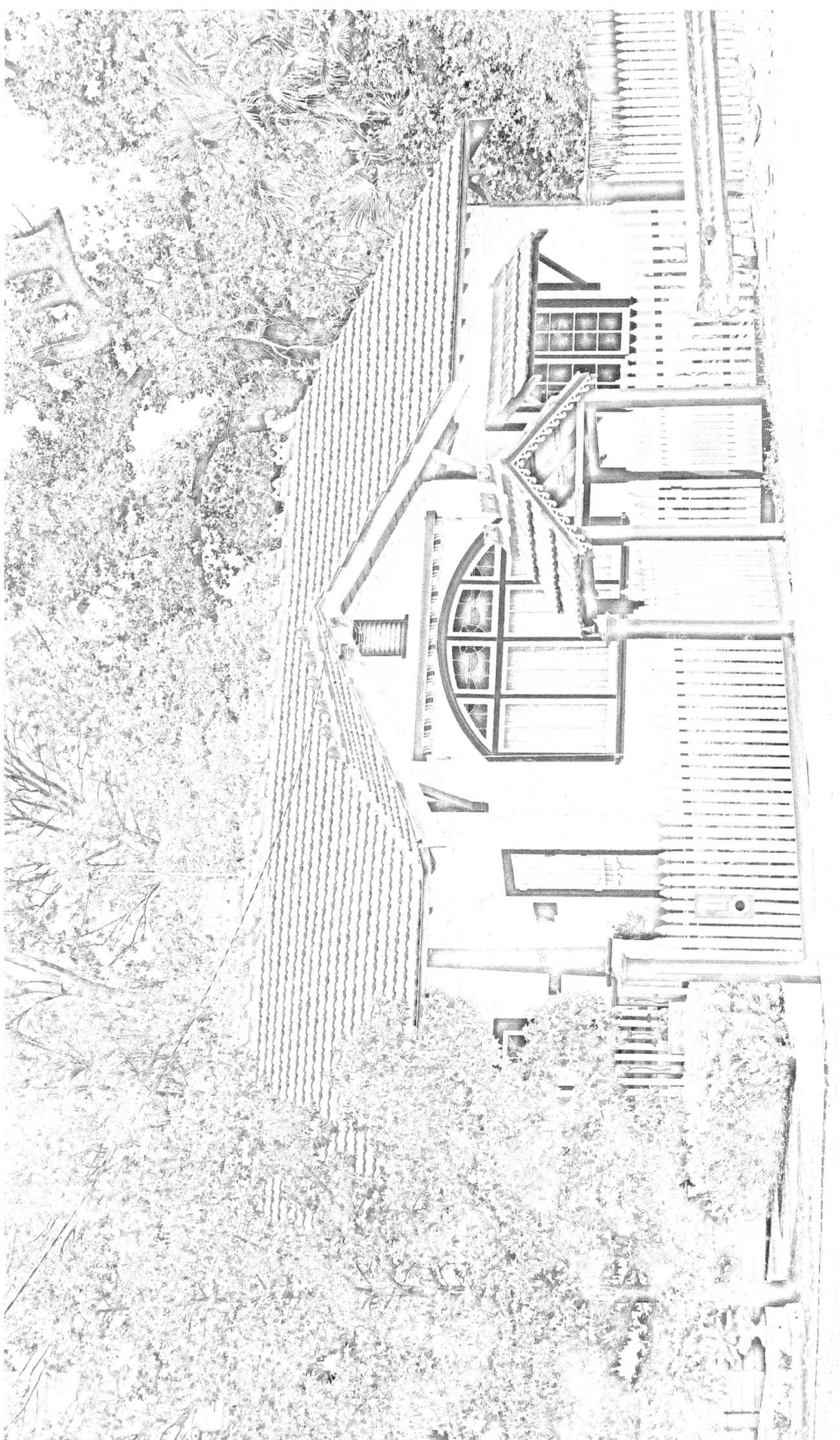

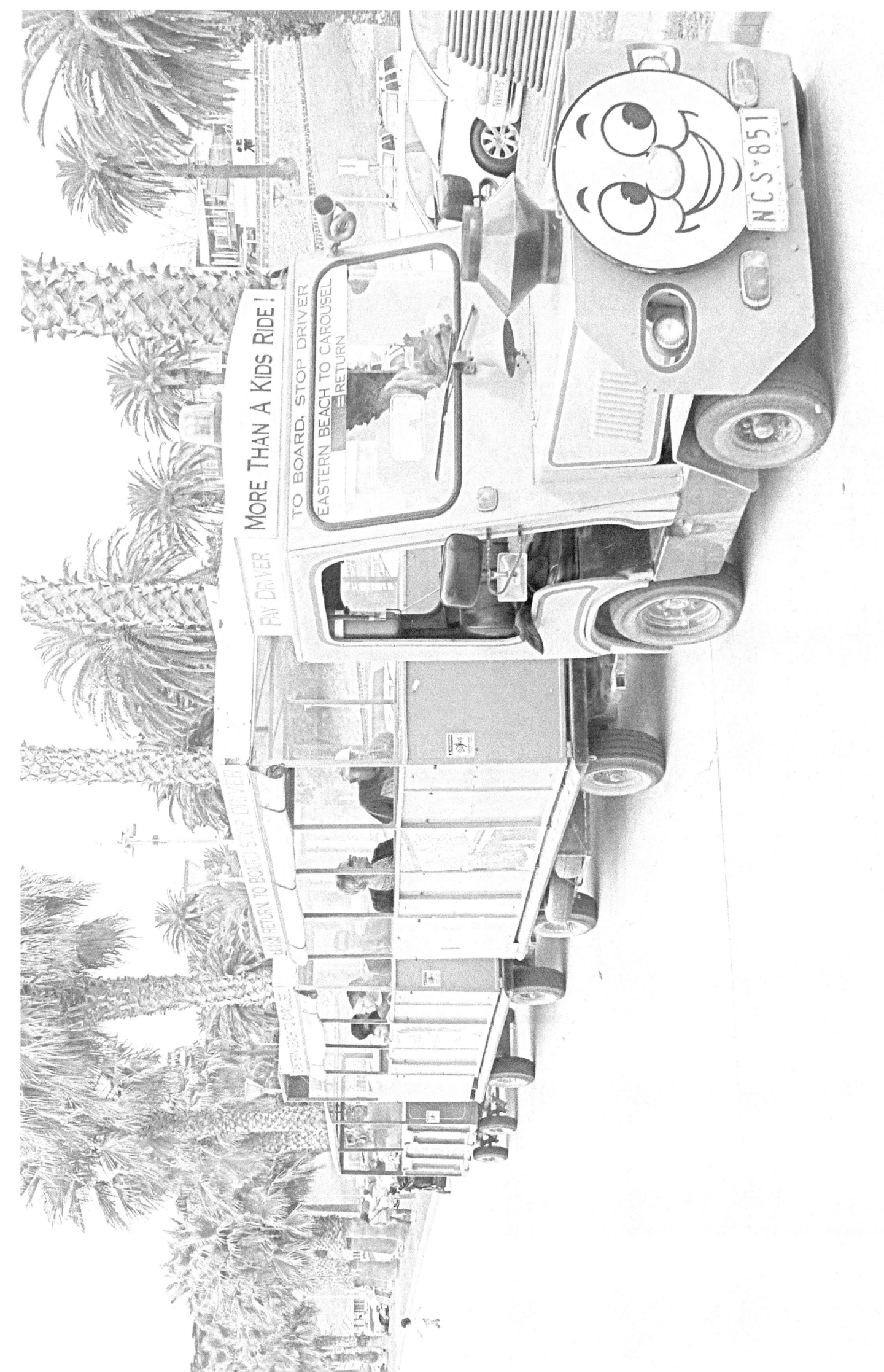

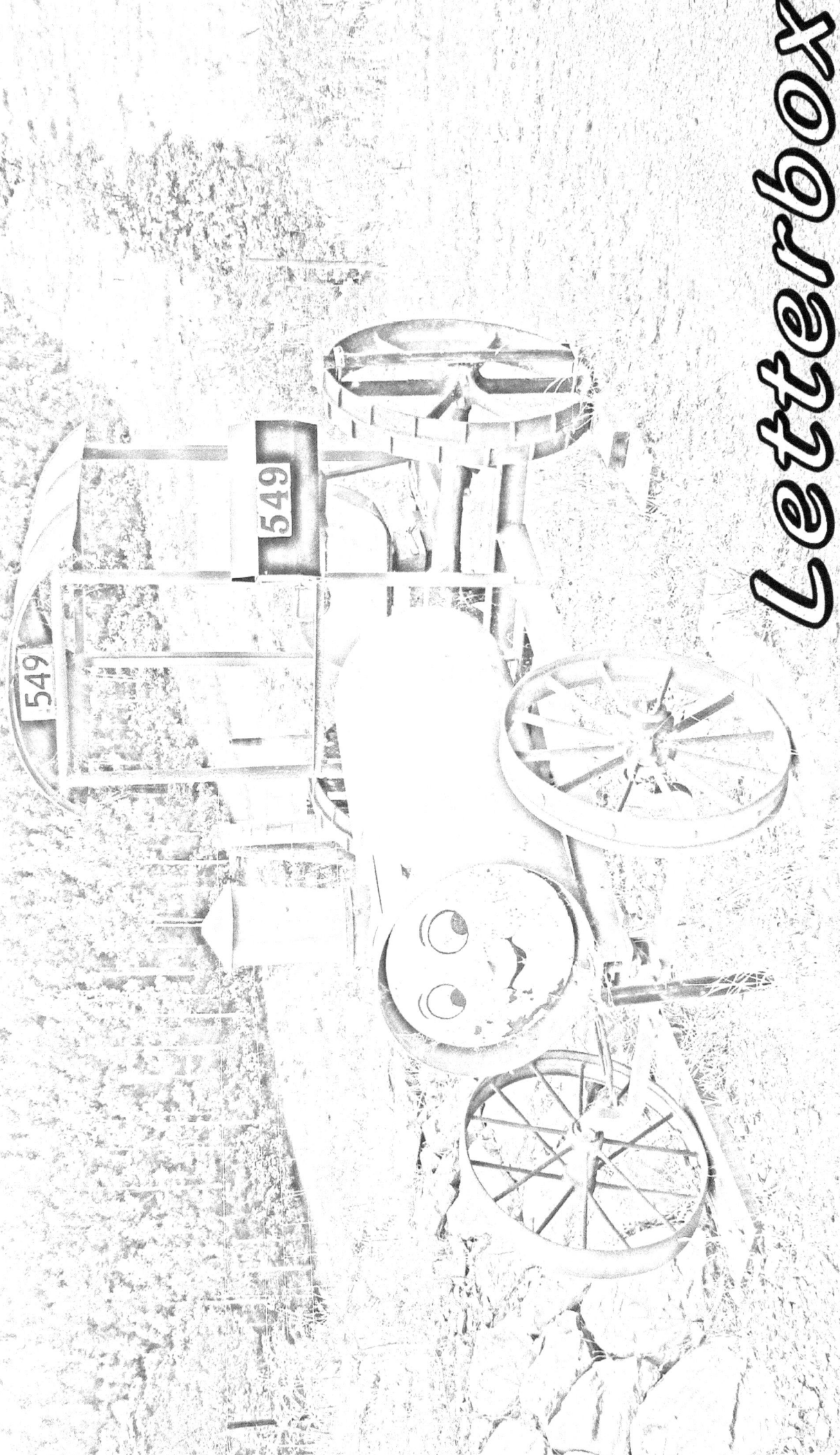

Letterbox

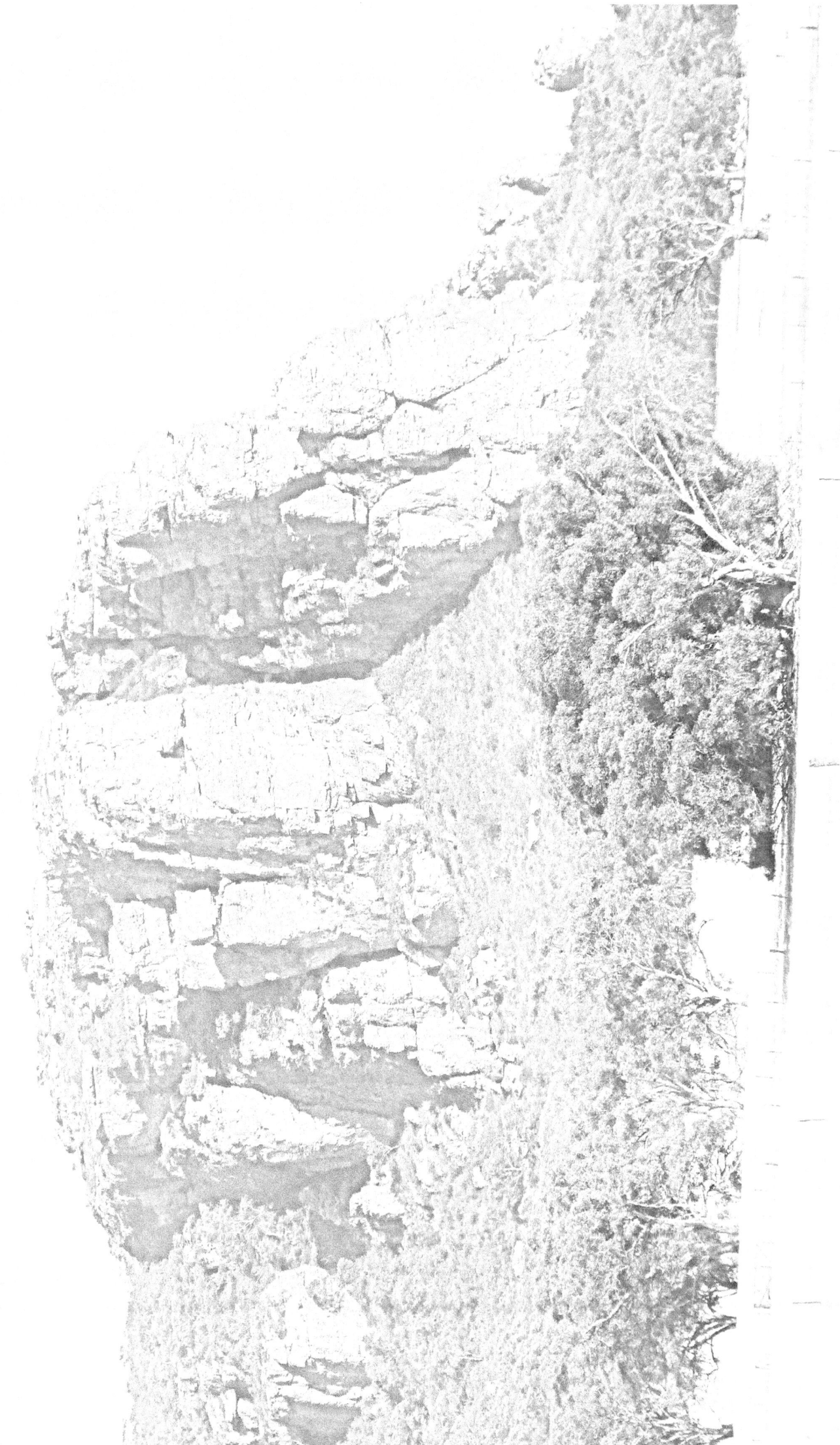

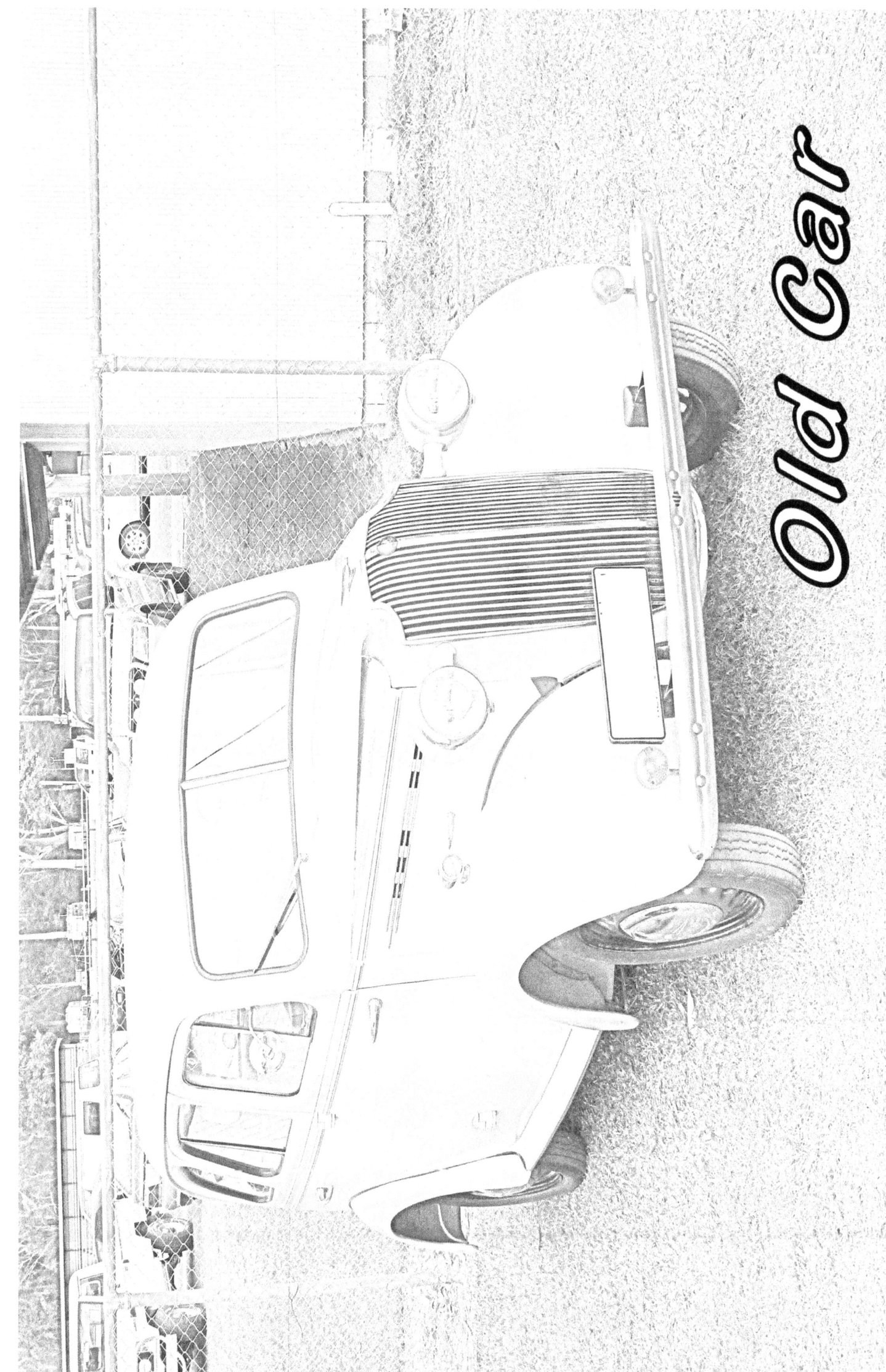

Old Car

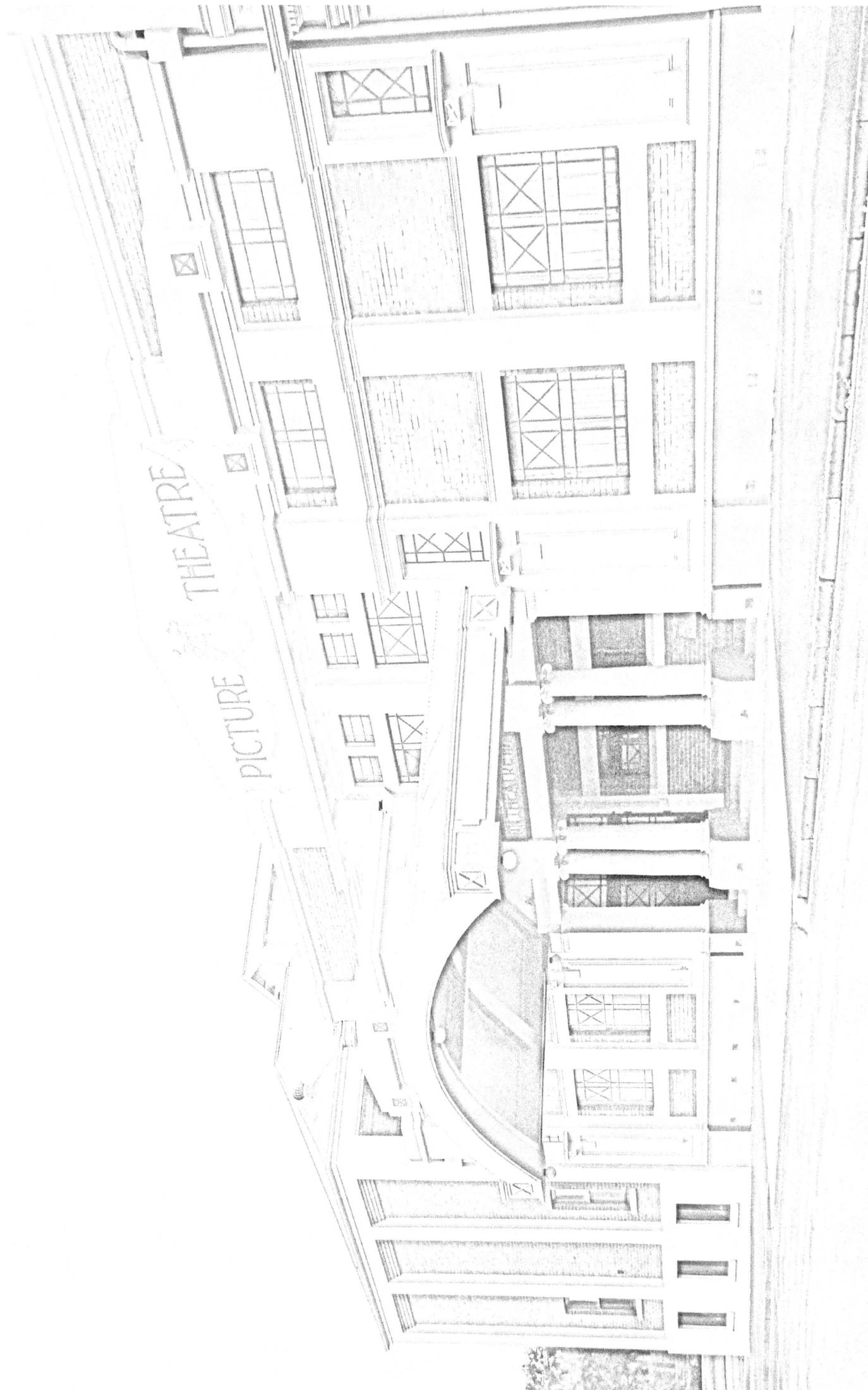

Pelicans

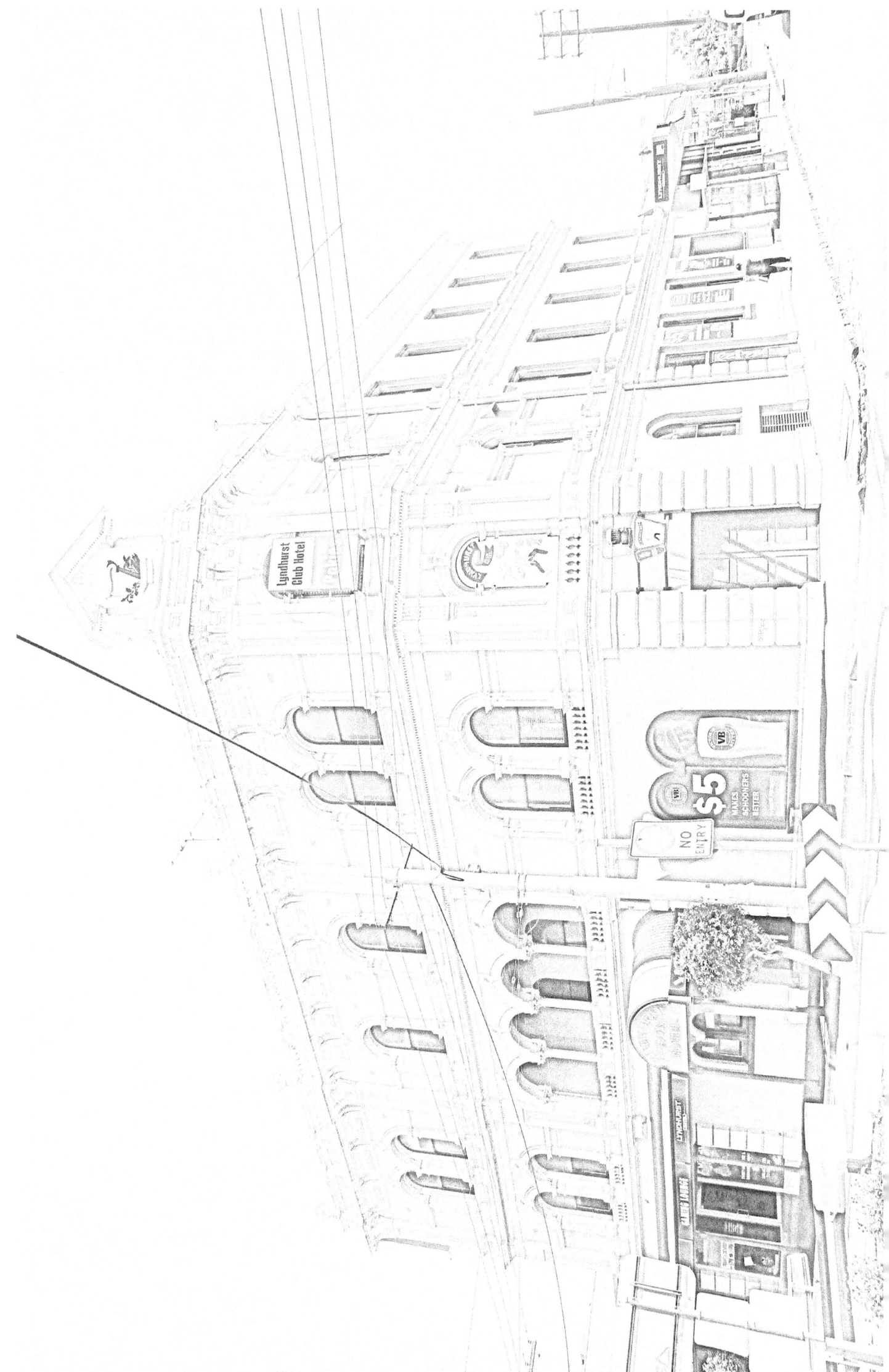

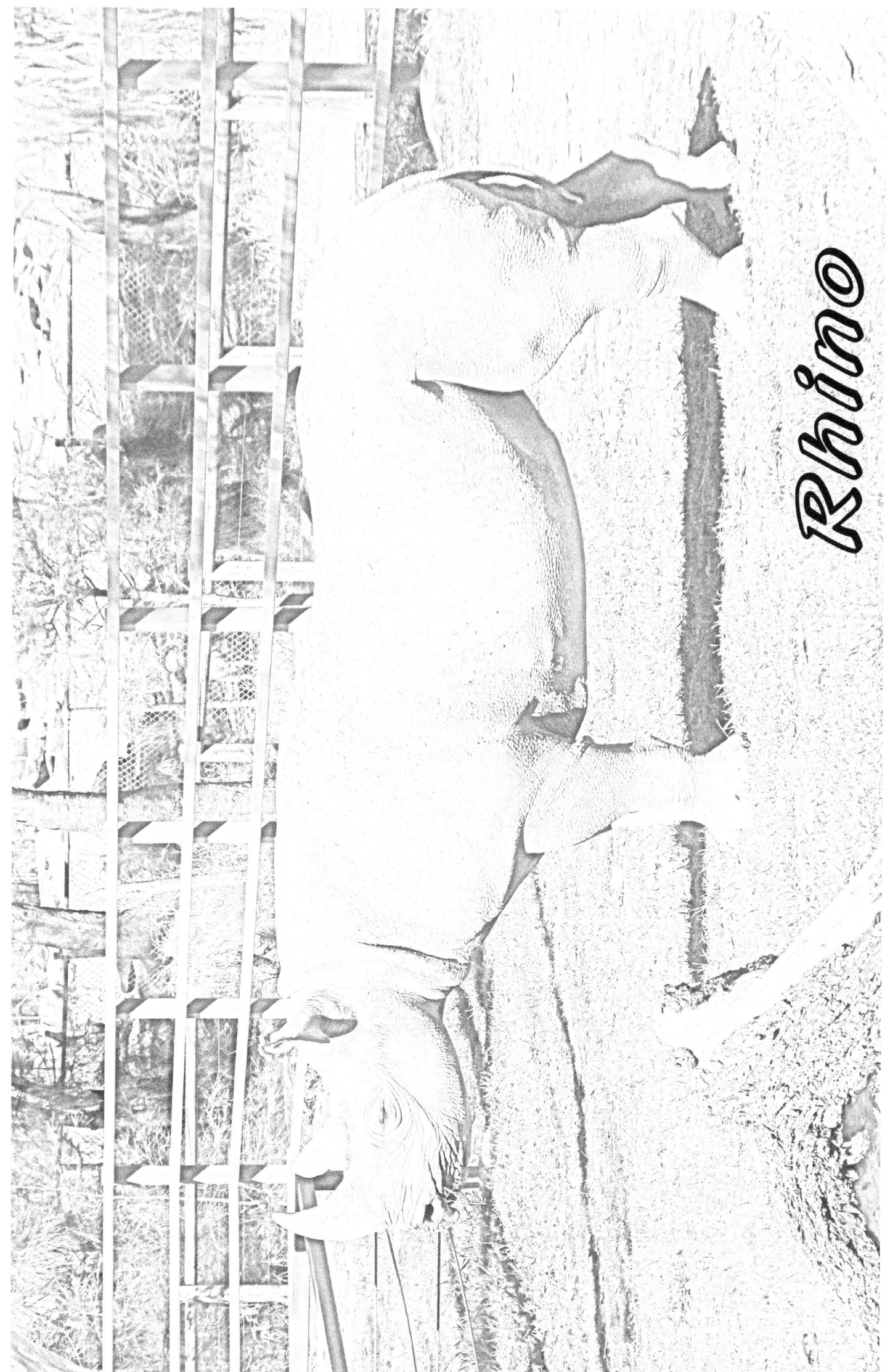

Rhino

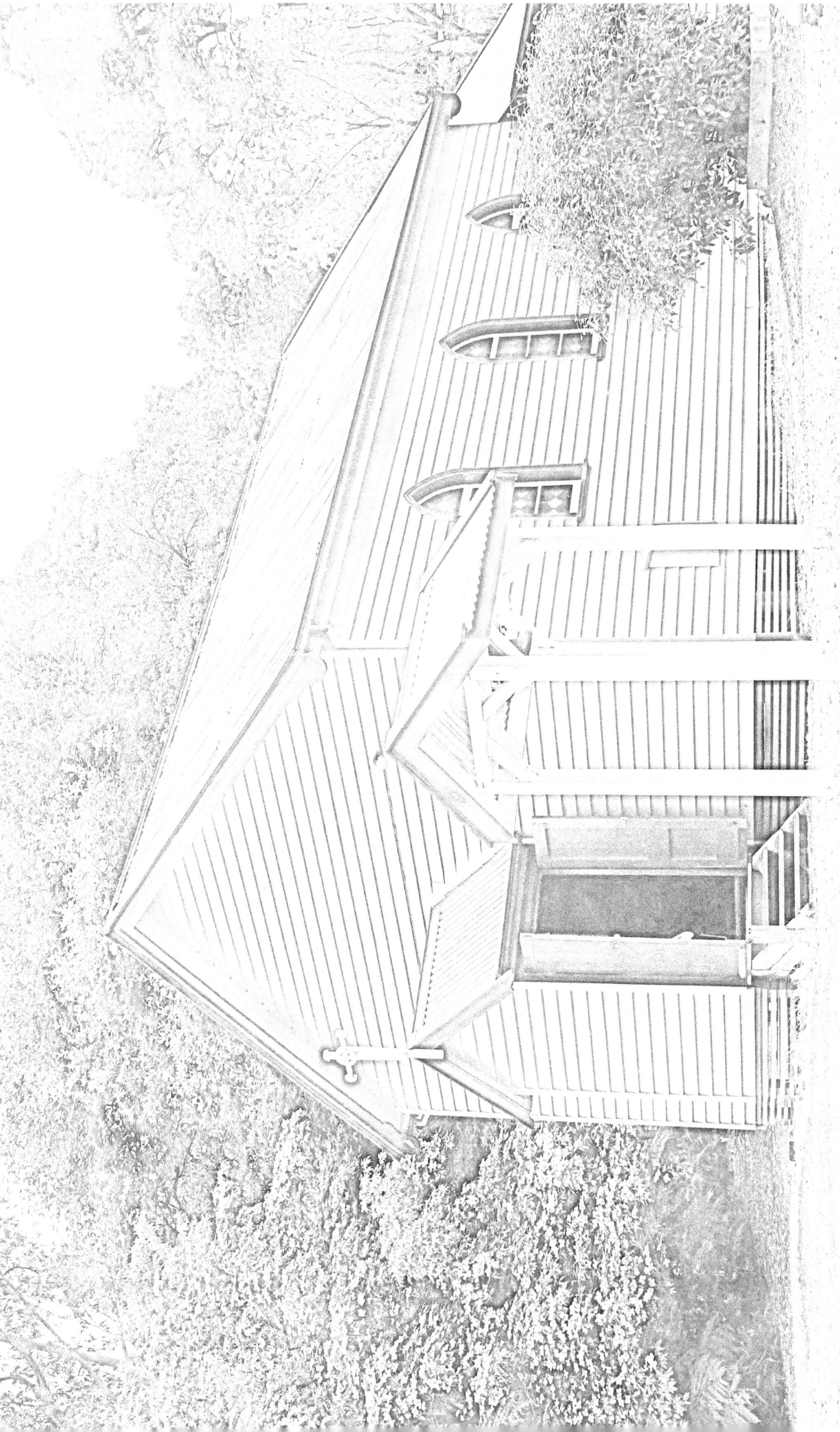

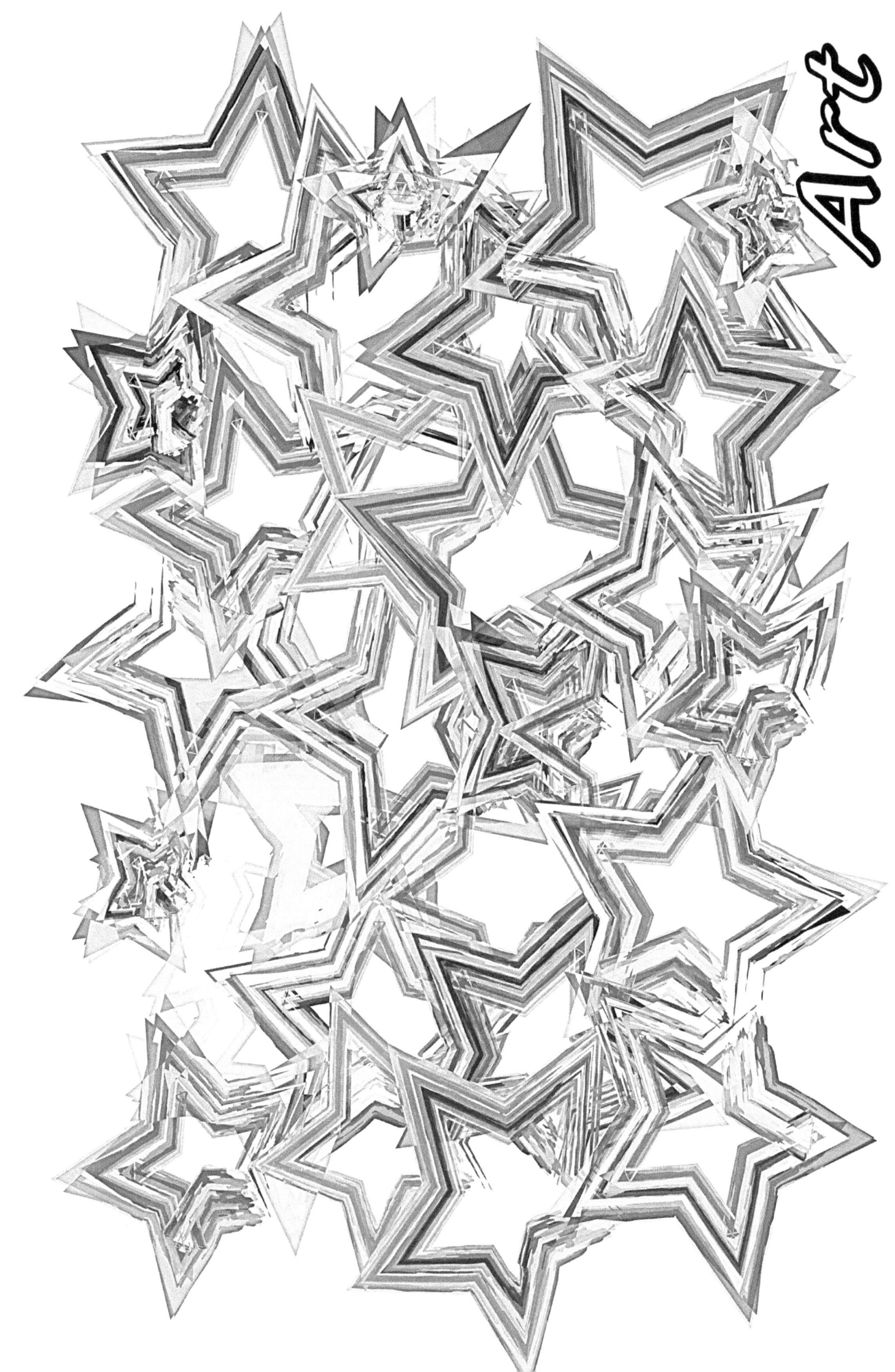

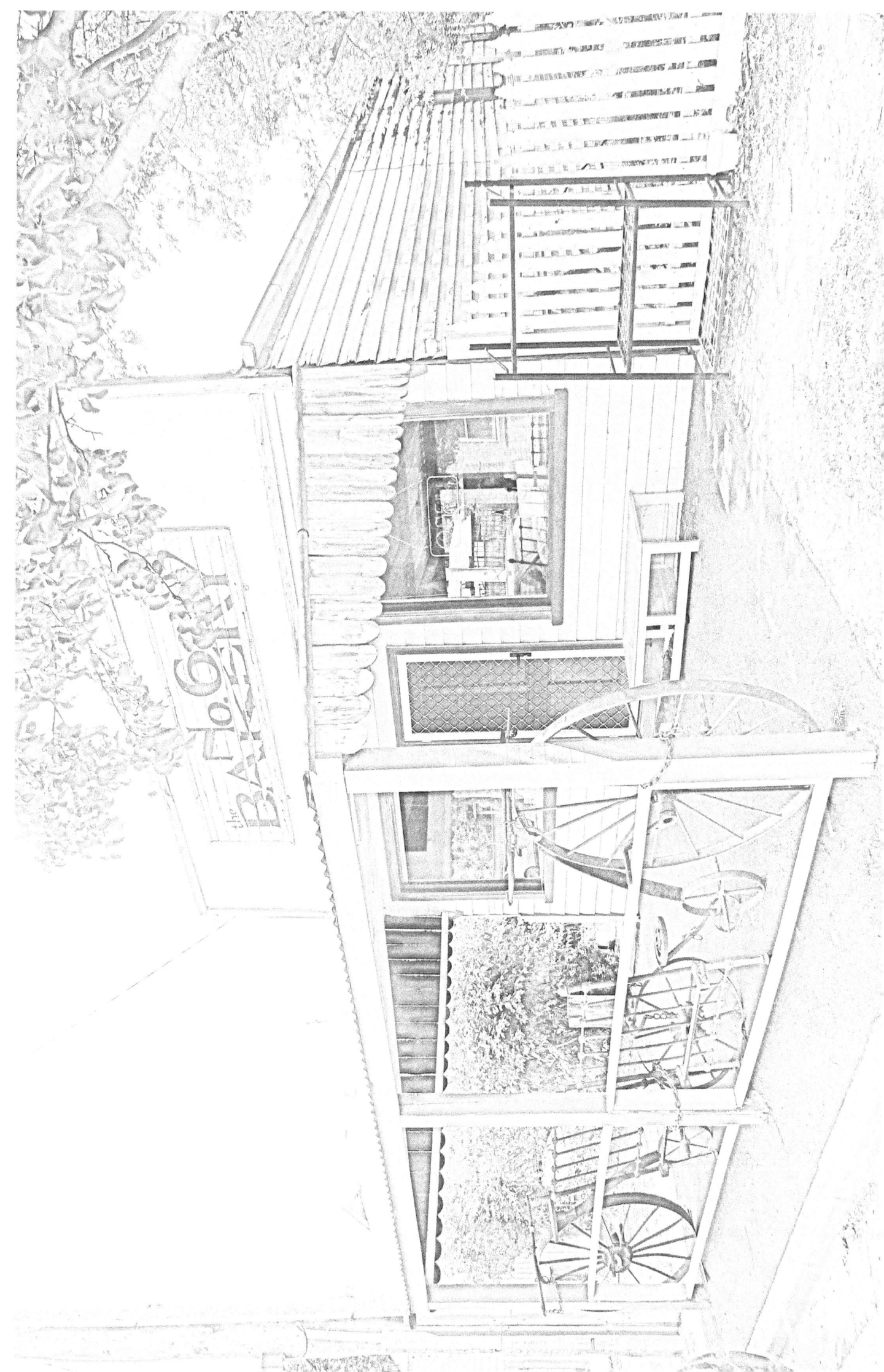

Soldier Crabs

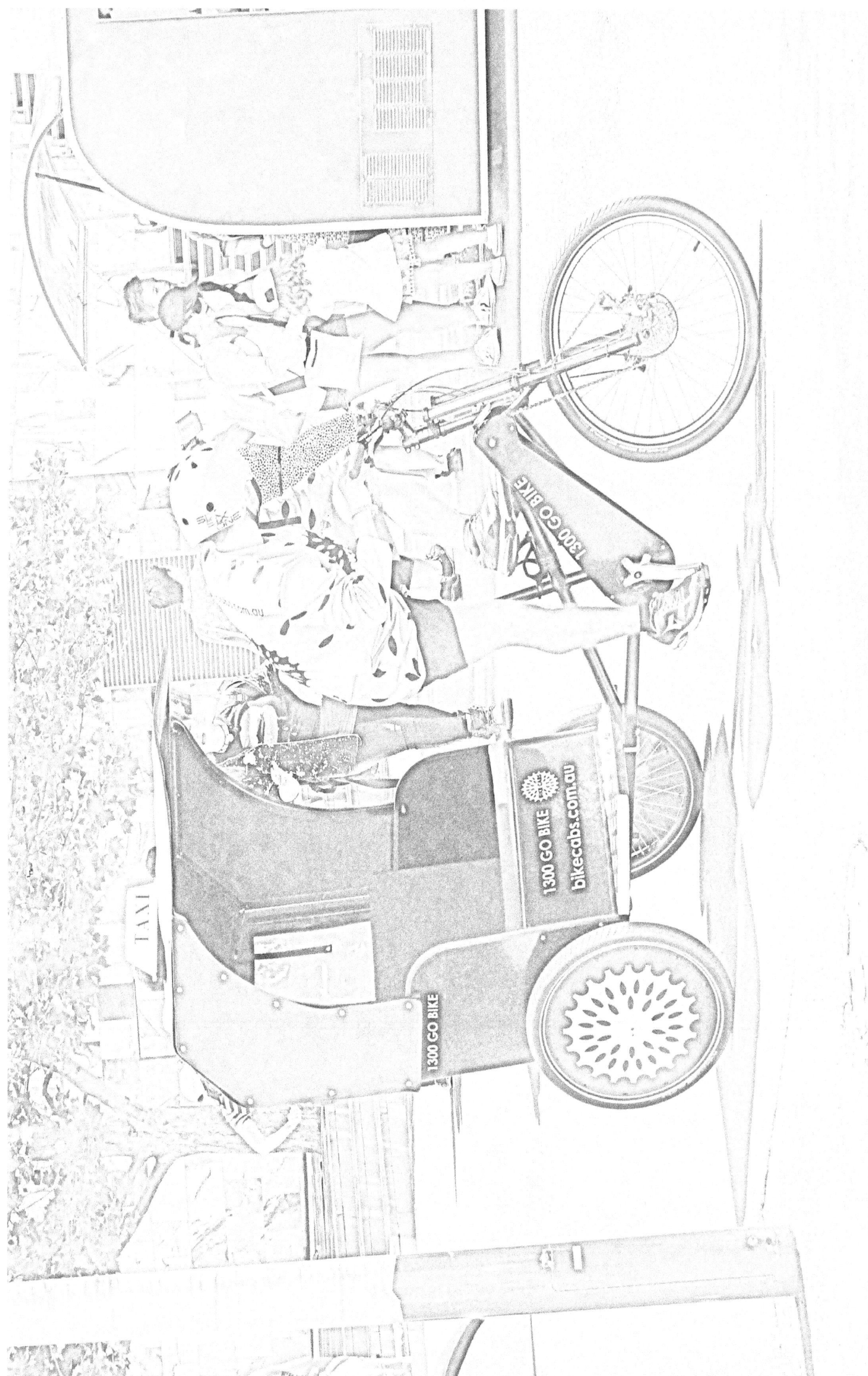

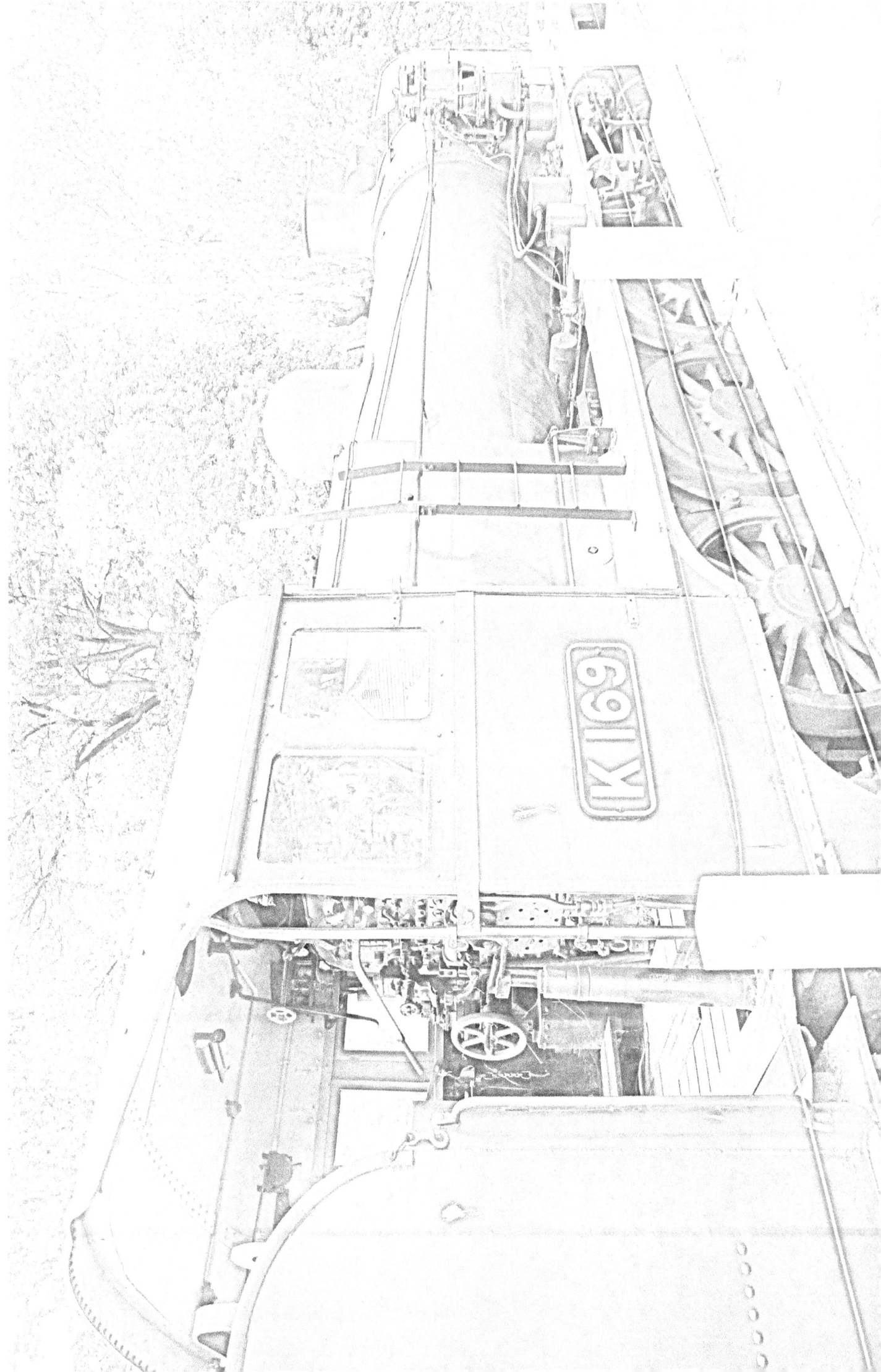

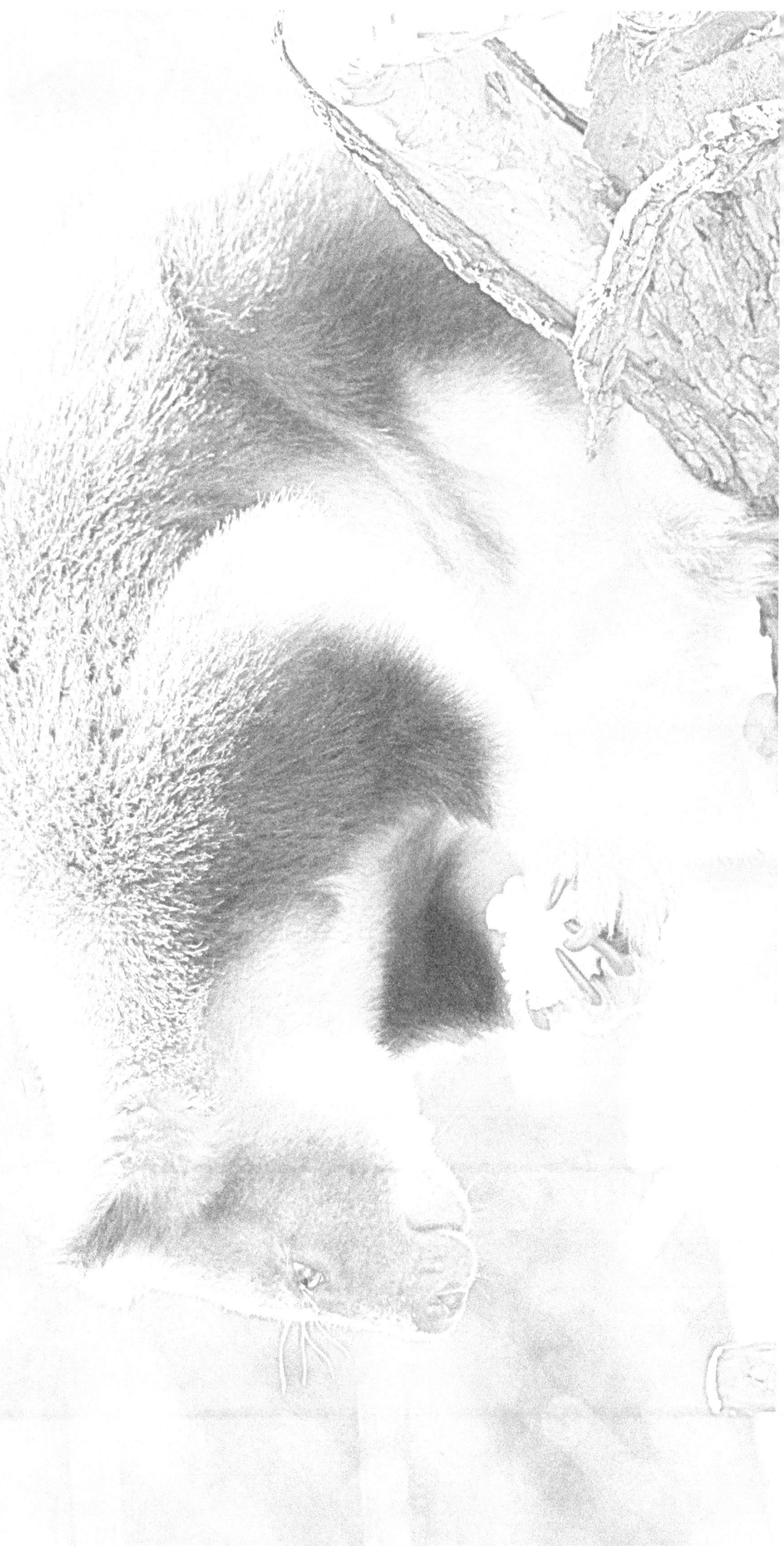

Tree Kangaroo

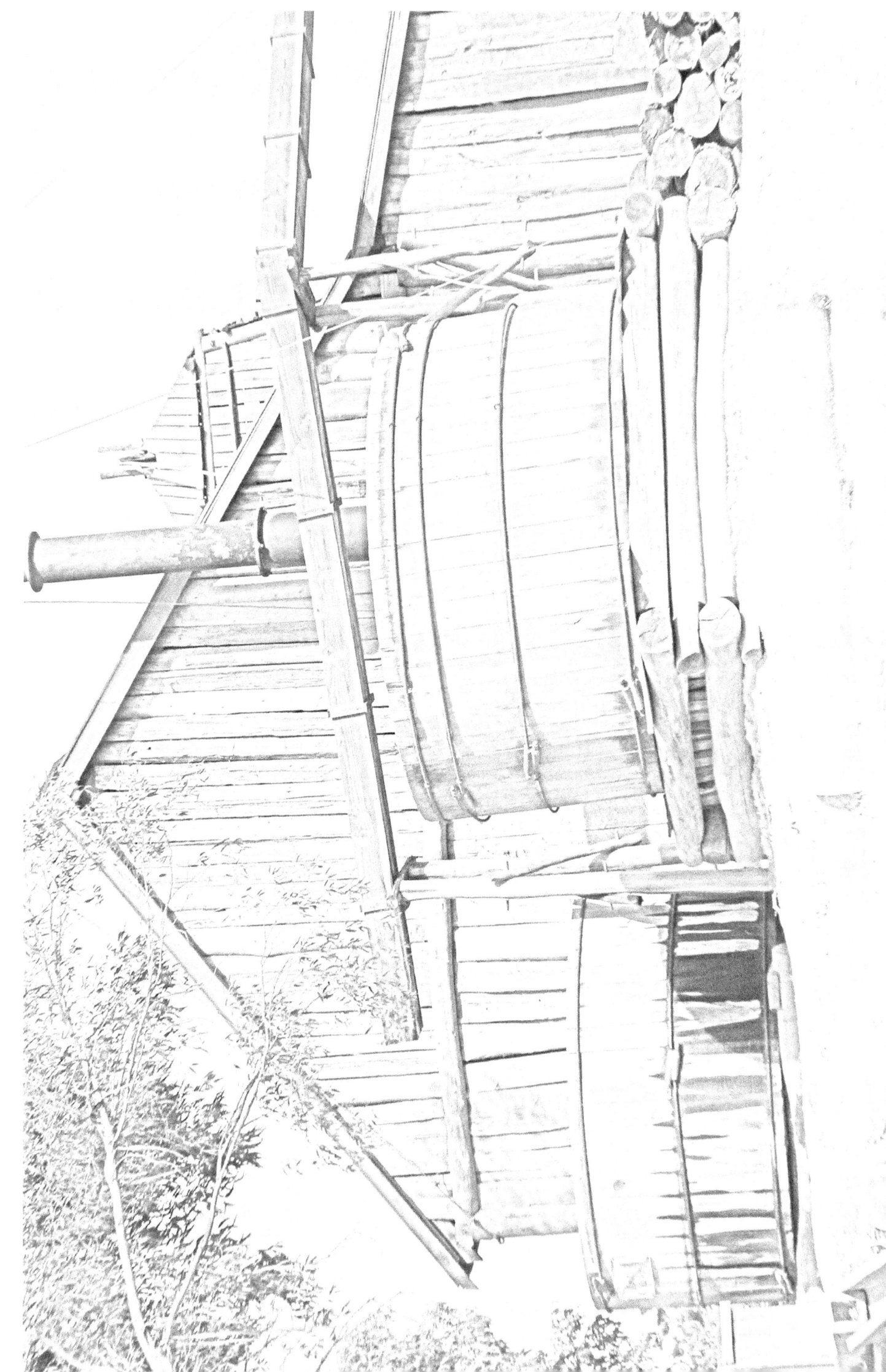

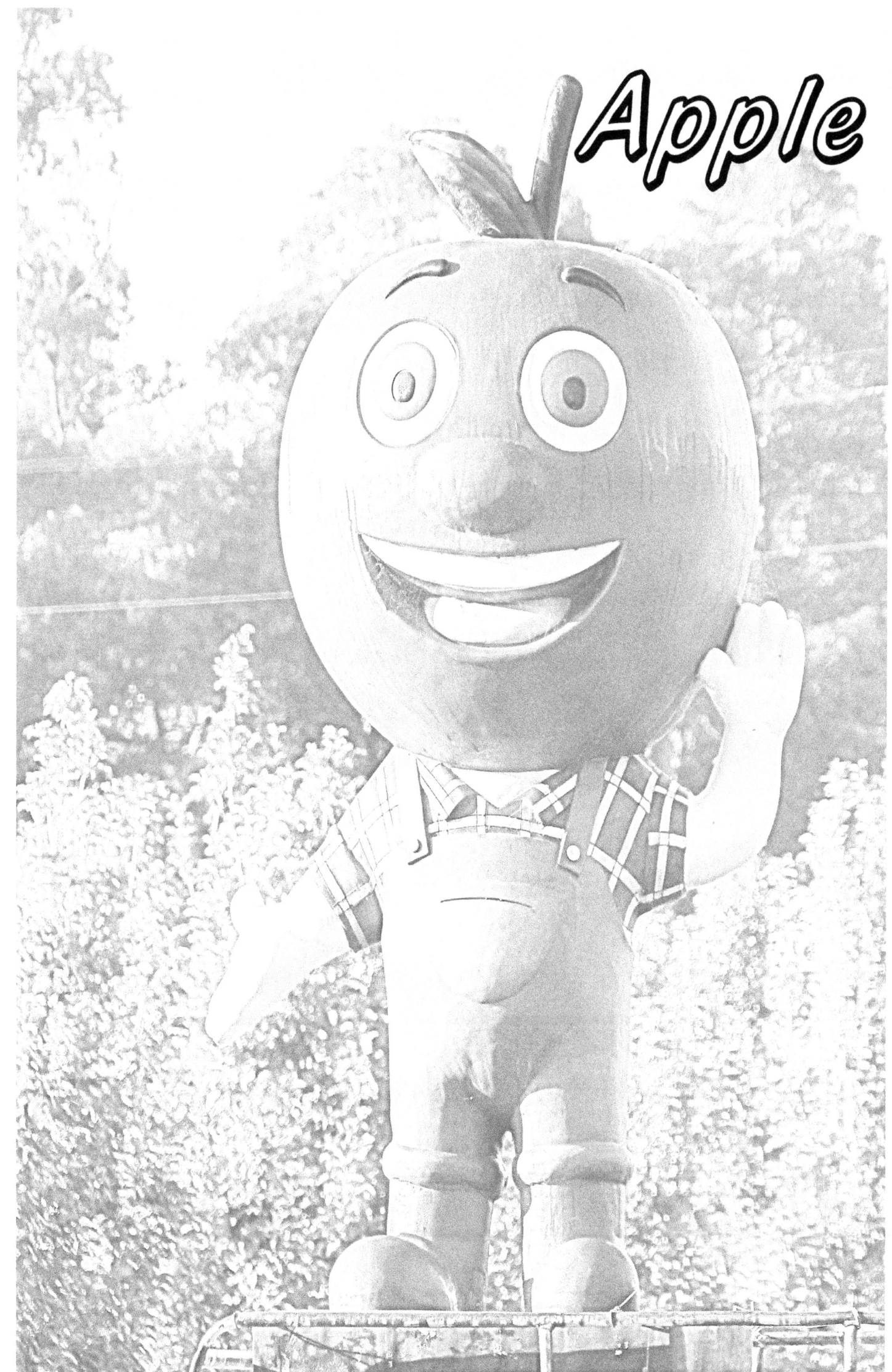

Apple

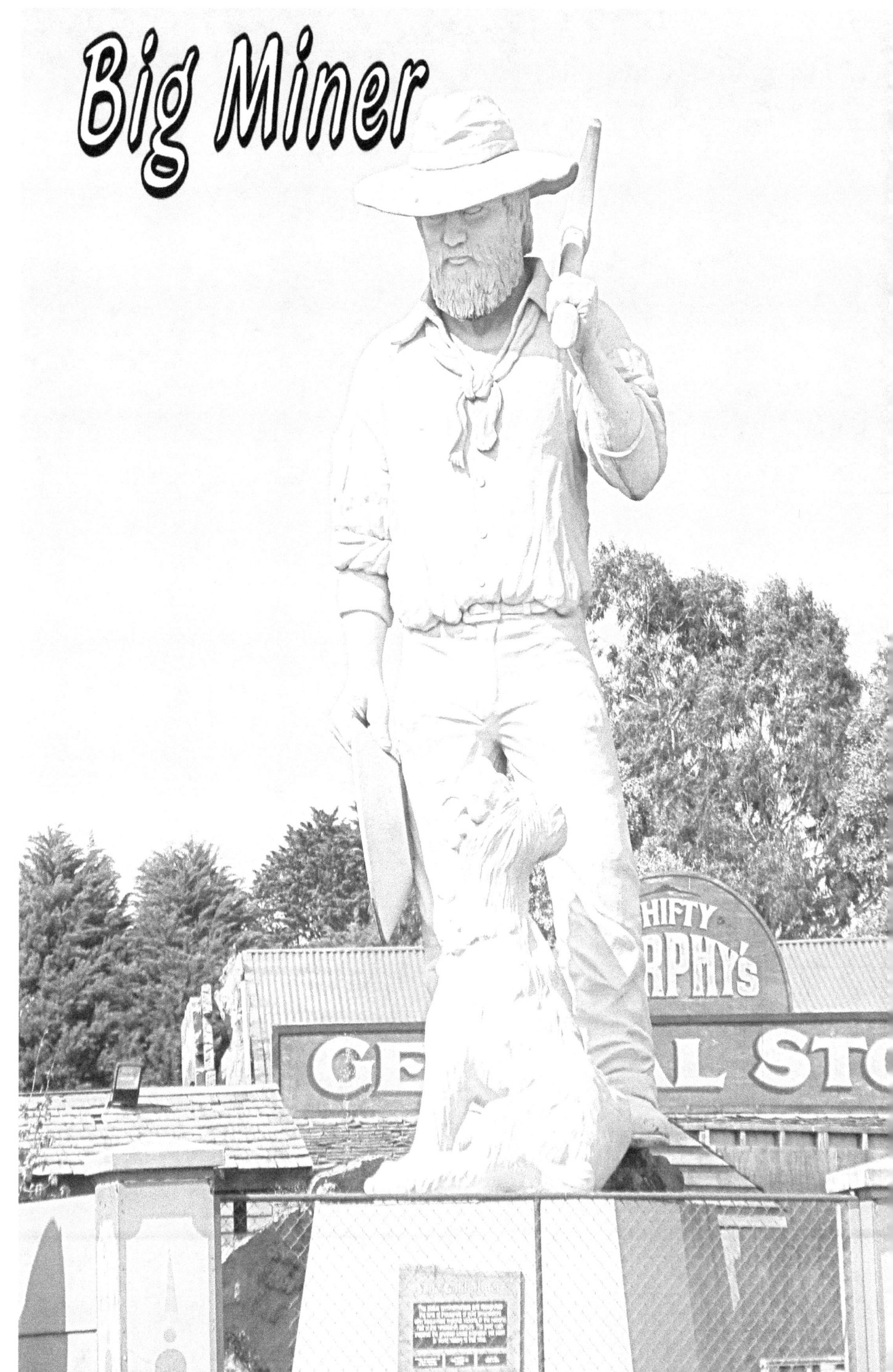

Big Miner

Dog

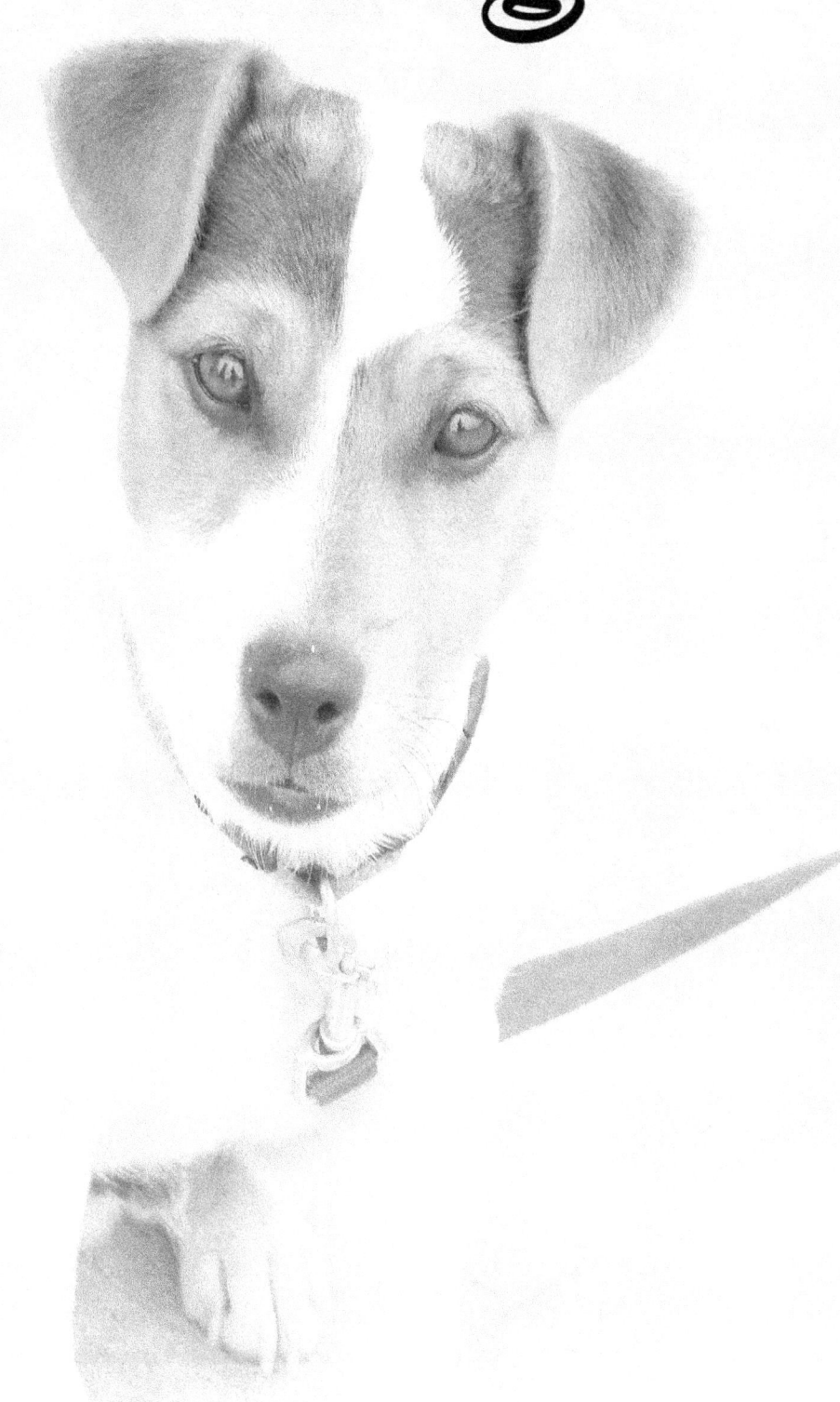

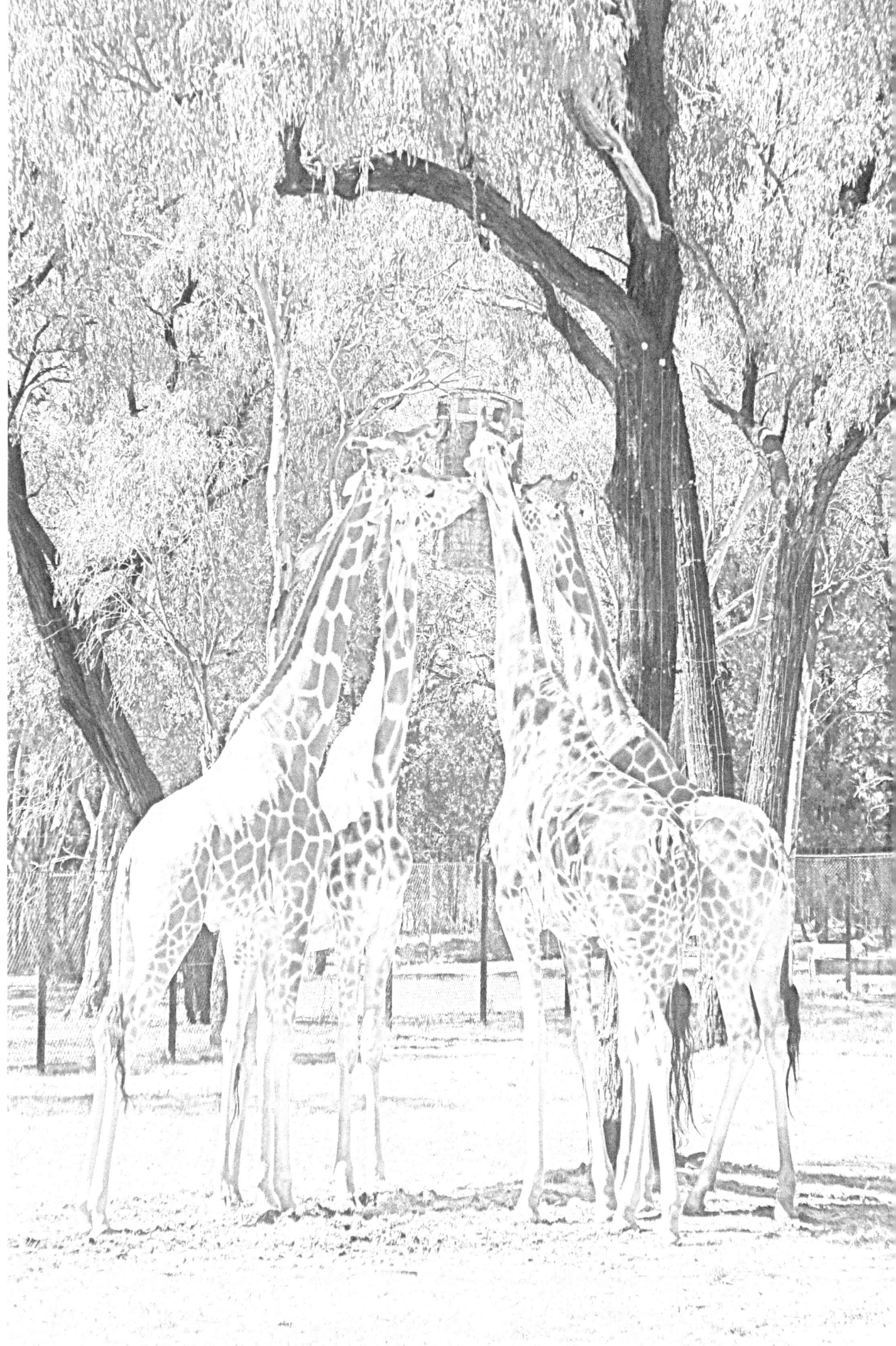

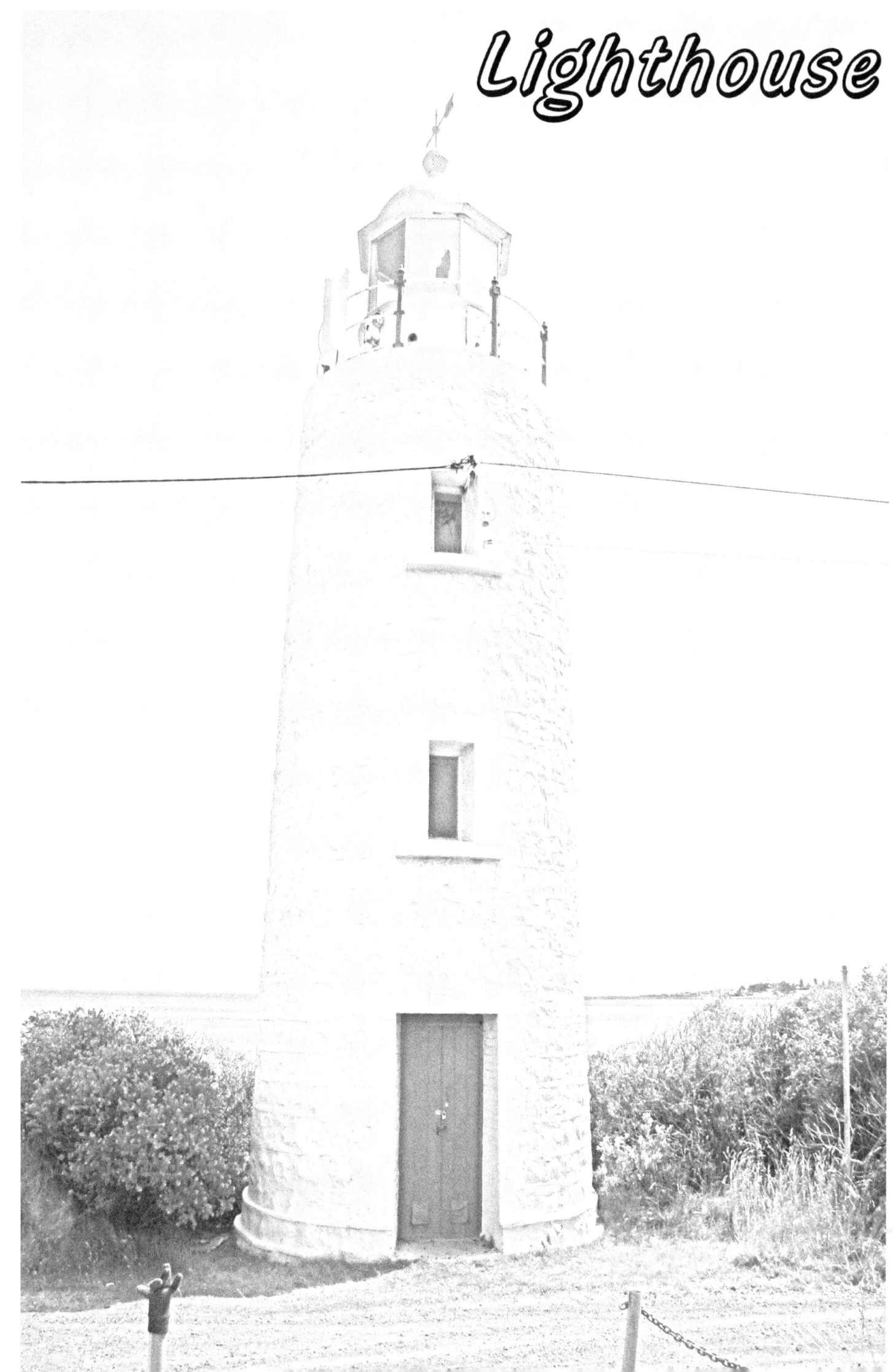

Lighthouse

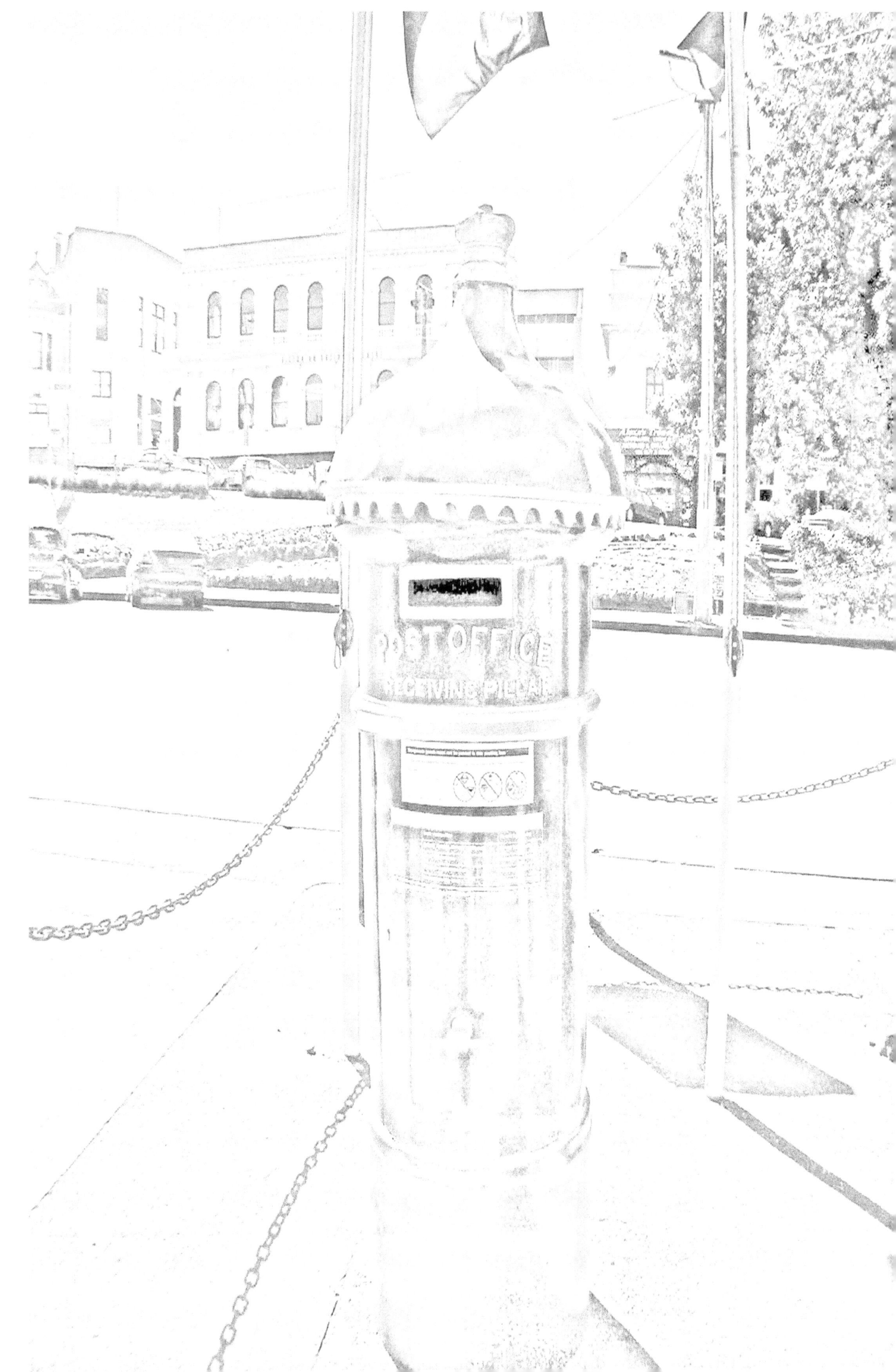

Monkey